Praise for *Azure AI Services at Scale for Cloud, Mobile, and Edge*

Creating modern applications powered by machine learning and AI is too hard, even when you have the tools at hand to do it. In this book, Bisson, Branscombe, Hoder, and Anand show how much simpler it can be, with up-to-date and clear guidance on how to use the capabilities already built into Azure.

—*John Montgomery, CVP, Azure AI Products, Microsoft*

This book is an easy read for anyone looking to understand what Microsoft's AI services can do for them, how to use the AI services in their business and applications, and how they should use AI responsibly for good. Highly recommended for anyone looking to build intelligent applications at scale using Microsoft Azure AI services.

—*Sundar Srinivasan, VP,*
Search Technology Center India (STCI), Microsoft

An invaluable introduction to Microsoft's family of AI services, with the added bonus of a thought-provoking section on using AI responsibly. A genuine something for everyone reference. Recommended without reservation.

—*Rik Hepworth, Chief Consulting Officer, Black Marble*

This book on Azure AI services is a must read for anyone looking for guidance on building intelligent applications and implementing an AI-oriented architecture for their organizations. Congratulations to the authors for delivering an insightful AI book that has fused the nuts and bolts of AI with years of practical on-the-ground experience.

—*Wee Hyong Tok, O'Reilly Book Author*
and Principal GPM, Microsoft

The time has clearly come for building AI-oriented applications, to tap into their immense potential, and to do so in a trustworthy, responsible way. This book lays out a compelling path that will help innovators create the next generation of intelligent systems using Azure's popular AI services in a way that will be both highly effective and sustainable.

—*Dion Hinchcliffe, VP and Principal Analyst,*
Constellation Research

This book is a one-stop-shop for what, how, why, and "whether you should" questions for those looking to benefit from the democratization of AI offered by Microsoft's cloud services.

—*Eric Boyd, CVP, Azure AI Platform, Microsoft*

Azure AI Services at Scale for Cloud, Mobile, and Edge

Building Intelligent Apps with Azure Cognitive Services and Machine Learning

Simon Bisson, Mary Branscombe, Chris Hoder, and Anand Raman

Beijing · Boston · Farnham · Sebastopol · Tokyo

Azure AI Services at Scale for Cloud, Mobile, and Edge

by Simon Bisson, Mary Branscombe, Chris Hoder, and Anand Raman

Copyright © 2022 O'Reilly Media, Inc. All rights reserved.

Published by O'Reilly Media, Inc., 1005 Gravenstein Highway North, Sebastopol, CA 95472.

O'Reilly books may be purchased for educational, business, or sales promotional use. Online editions are also available for most titles (*http://oreilly.com*). For more information, contact our corporate/institutional sales department: 800-998-9938 or corporate@oreilly.com.

Acquisitions Editor: Rebecca Novack	**Indexer:** Ellen Troutman-Zaig
Development Editor: Gary O'Brien	**Interior Designer:** David Futato
Production Editor: Beth Kelly	**Cover Designer:** Karen Montgomery
Copyeditor: nSight, Inc.	**Illustrator:** Kate Dullea
Proofreader: Piper Editorial Consulting, LLC	

April 2022:   First Edition

Revision History for the First Edition

2022-04-11:   First Release

See *http://oreilly.com/catalog/errata.csp?isbn=9781098108045* for release details.

978-1-098-10804-5

[LSI]

Table of Contents

Part III. AI-Oriented Architectures in the Real World

Preface

AI covers a wide range of techniques and approaches, and you'll find it everywhere from smartphones to the factory floor.

As AI advances, these techniques are becoming more powerful—and more complex to implement. Increasingly, the most powerful AI systems are being driven by very large deep learning models, trained on huge amounts of data, using billions of parameters that are then customized to solve specific problems.

Building and training those very large models takes the resources of a very large company with a lot of technical expertise—and a huge investment in the infrastructure to run them on. Training the GPT-3 language generation model developed by OpenAI cost on the order of $4 million or more. Just the initial training run on the 45 TB of data used for GPT-3 would take maybe a month of continuous training and over a thousand high-end graphics processing unit (GPU) cards.

That means only a handful of organizations in the world can create and run these very large models, which Stanford's Institute for Human-Centered Artificial Intelligence dubs foundation models because they're so significant to the way AI is currently being developed and used—and because you can build on them to create new systems.[1]

These include so-called large language models like GPT-3 but also extremely large machine learning models in many domains that rely on semi-supervised deep learning, self-supervised pretraining, transfer learning, and similar methods for creating large powerful models trained on powerful hardware using huge datasets that can then be applied to a variety of problems or custom trained to work on very specific problems.

---

[1] See *On the Opportunities and Risks of Foundation Models* (*https://arxiv.org/pdf/2108.07258.pdf*) for an extensive and thought-provoking analysis of the advantages and possible dangers of this increasingly common approach.

Even a business with the expertise to build a deep learning system might find models too expensive to train and run in production themselves, especially when they need to do more work to mitigate bias in models trained on imperfectly curated datasets drawn from the open web to implement them responsibly. But anyone can take advantage of very large foundational models and even customize them for their own needs by using the Azure AI services that Microsoft makes available in the cloud.

Other techniques, like reinforcement learning, have only just emerged from research labs and require significant expertise to implement.

With Azure AI services, you can rely on the scale of development, training, and deployment that the public cloud brings and spend your time building an app or workflow that solves a problem for your users.

Who This Book Is For

The cloud AI services Azure provides bring a wide range of the latest developments to any developer and even to business users, as well as data scientists and data engineers.

There are so many techniques and so many places you might want to use AI that even organizations who are hiring and training data engineers and data scientists want to make them more productive by using AI cloud services. Cloud services also unlock the possibilities of AI for developers and business experts who will never be data engineers or data scientists.

There are so many different AI tools and services from Microsoft that run on Azure that we can't cover them all in depth, so we've picked out four key areas. The Power Platform helps business users and professional developers alike build apps and workflows that take advantage of AI. Azure Cognitive Services and Applied AI Services give developers APIs, software development kits (SDKs), and ready-made solutions to incorporate in their code. Azure Machine Learning is powerful enough for data scientists but also has options that help people who aren't AI experts to train their own models to solve their particular business problems.

The worlds of AI and cloud services are both fast moving, so what we can capture in this book is the principles behind them, the best practices that will make you successful, and examples of what you can achieve. In particular, we look at how to use AI responsibly: a question of increasing importance for many developers.

We cover the practical, hands-on side of using some key features across the range of services, but bear in mind that those services may have been updated by the time you come to use them. The steps we describe might be slightly different from what you see in the cloud services, performance may have improved, and you will likely find extra features that let you achieve even more!

How to Use This Book

In this book, we want to help you get started with cloud AI services, whatever your background or your level of familiarity with Azure. If you're not familiar with how powerful AI techniques and machine learning models have become, Chapter 1 looks at the current state of the art, including the key research milestones that Azure AI is built on.

To learn about the whole range of AI tools and services available as part of Microsoft's AI platform, turn to Chapter 2 where we look at the many different choices you can make—including bringing cloud AI into your own infrastructure if you need to run at the edge.

If you have an idea for what you want to build and how Azure AI services can help you, you can jump straight into Part II.

If you're an experienced developer and you're ready to get started on building machine learning models straight away, begin with Chapter 3, where we look at Azure Machine Learning, Microsoft's comprehensive machine learning service in the cloud where you can work with industry standard frameworks like PyTorch and TensorFlow.

If you'd rather call APIs to take advantage of prebuilt models that you can fine-tune for common AI tasks or entire scenarios, using a variety of familiar programming languages and your favorite developer tools, go straight to Chapters 4 and 5, where we cover Azure Cognitive Services and Azure Applied AI Services.

But you don't have to be a developer to use Azure AI. Many Azure Cognitive Services are available in the low-code Power Platform and in the no-code AI Builder tool. In Chapter 6, we walk you through how anyone can use machine learning to understand data and solve problems.

If you want to take a step back and think about how you're going to use AI, where your data is going to come from, and how to do all of that responsibly, turn to Chapters 7 and 8, where we look at the ethical approaches and best practices that will help you make the most of cloud AI.

Want to be sure cloud AI can really scale to handle your problems, however large and complex? Thinking it might make more sense to run your own AI infrastructure? In Chapter 9, we go behind the scenes of Azure Cognitive Services and look at what it means to run a worldwide, 24-7 API platform with dozens of machine learning models in production—and keep it always up to date.

Part III continues by looking at how other organizations are using Azure AI services to describe the world to blind users, pick exactly the right products to recommend even when buying habits changed overnight because of the pandemic, and translate speech between multiple languages in real time. In Chapters 10, 11, and 12, we have case studies of real-world systems built with AI-oriented architectures that integrate different Azure AI services to show you what's possible.

But with Azure AI, the real limit is your imagination—and the data you can bring to the problem. Read on for ideas about what you can do and how you can get started.

Conventions Used in This Book

The following typographical conventions are used in this book:

Italic
> Indicates new terms, URLs, email addresses, filenames, and file extensions.

`Constant width`
> Used for program listings, as well as within paragraphs to refer to program elements such as variable or function names, databases, data types, environment variables, statements, and keywords.

`Constant width bold`
> Shows commands or other text that should be typed literally by the user.

`Constant width italic`
> Shows text that should be replaced with user-supplied values or by values determined by context.

This element signifies a tip or suggestion.

This element signifies a general note.

This element indicates a warning or caution.

Using Code Examples

You can download the supplemental material for this book, like code samples, from *https://github.com/Azure-Samples/Azure-AI-Services-O-reilly-book-Companion-repo*.

This book is here to help you get the most from the Azure AI services. In general, if example code is offered with this book, you may use it in your programs and documentation. You do not need to contact us for permission unless you're reproducing a significant portion of the code. For example, writing a program that uses several chunks of code from this book does not require permission. Selling or distributing a CD-ROM of examples from O'Reilly books does require permission. Answering a question by citing this book and quoting example code does not require permission. Incorporating a significant amount of example code from this book into your product's documentation does require permission.

We appreciate, but do not require, attribution. An attribution usually includes the title, author, publisher, and ISBN. For example: "*Azure AI Services at Scale for Cloud, Mobile, and Edge* by Simon Bisson, Mary Branscombe, Chris Hoder, and Anand Raman (O'Reilly). Copyright 2022 O'Reilly Media, Inc., 978-1-098-10804-5."

If you feel your use of code examples falls outside fair use or the permission given above, feel free to contact us at *permissions@oreilly.com*.

O'Reilly Online Learning

 For more than 40 years, *O'Reilly Media* has provided technology and business training, knowledge, and insight to help companies succeed.

Our unique network of experts and innovators share their knowledge and expertise through books, articles, and our online learning platform. O'Reilly's online learning platform gives you on-demand access to live training courses, in-depth learning paths, interactive coding environments, and a vast collection of text and video from O'Reilly and 200+ other publishers. For more information, visit *https://oreilly.com*.

How to Contact Us

Please address comments and questions concerning this book to the publisher:

O'Reilly Media, Inc.
1005 Gravenstein Highway North
Sebastopol, CA 95472
800-998-9938 (in the United States or Canada)

707-829-0515 (international or local)
707-829-0104 (fax)

We have a web page for this book, where we list errata, examples, and any additional information. You can access this page at *https://oreil.ly/azure-ai*.

Email *bookquestions@oreilly.com* to comment or ask technical questions about this book.

For news and information about our books and courses, visit *https://oreilly.com*.

Find us on LinkedIn: *https://linkedin.com/company/oreilly-media*

Follow us on Twitter: *https://twitter.com/oreillymedia*

Watch us on YouTube: *https://youtube.com/oreillymedia*

Acknowledgments

The authors may write the words, but it takes a lot more work to create a book, and this one wouldn't have been possible without many people who helped along the way.

For help with specific chapters, although of course all mistakes are our own, we're indebted to:

Chapter 3: Prashant Ketkar
Chapter 6: Amir Netz, Justyna Lucznik, Antoine Cellerier, Joe Fernandez
Chapter 7: Saleema Amershi, Sarah Bird, Mehrnoosh Sameki, Mihaela Vorvoreanu
Chapter 9: Greg Clark
Chapter 10: Saqib Shaik
Chapter 11: Ivo Ramos, Olivier Nano
Chapter 12: Jeff Mendenhall

This book also benefited immeasurably from the work of the team at O'Reilly: Gary O'Brien, Jonathan Hassell, Rebecca Novack, Beth Kelly, Kate Dullea, and Sharon Tripp.

From Mary Branscombe and Simon Bisson

Andrew Blake, Doug Burger, Lili Cheng, Katja Hoffman, Eric Horvitz, Charles Lamanna, Peter Lee, John Langford, James Phillips, Mark Russinovich, Dharma Shukla, Patrice Simard, Jeffrey Snover, John Winn, and the many others who have helped us understand machine learning techniques and Microsoft services over the years. And a tip of the hat to James Doran, emeritus professor at the University of Essex and Mary's MSc thesis supervisor, from whom she first heard the term "machine learning."

From Chris Hoder

All the amazing folks in the Cognitive Services and partner teams who made these services and this book possible and have helped me understand machine learning, applied AI, and numerous other invaluable things along the way. And to Lauren Hoder for her love and support.

From Anand Raman

My parents and sister for all the values they taught that made me the person I am today. My wife Anupama and kids Aashray and Ahana for their inspiration, love, and support every day. And all my colleagues at Microsoft who have helped me understand AI/machine learning and numerous other invaluable things along the way.

## PART I

Understanding AI-Oriented Architecture

## CHAPTER 1

An Introduction to AI-Oriented Architecture

What You Can Do with AI

The power of AI is doing what you couldn't do before, because it was too expensive or tedious for humans to do, or because they couldn't react quickly enough. AI can monitor a video feed of drivers at every gas station in a large chain to watch for safety issues like someone throwing away a lit cigarette. It can identify individual elephants in an endangered herd, predict failures in machinery before they happen, warn you which contracts are going to expire in the next 30 days across every area of your business, or pick the most promising drug formulation to test or the most enticing product to offer a customer.

AI can track millions of fishing boats and predict which of them might be breaking regulations designed to avoid overfishing or spot illegally trafficked ivory in a suitcase at the airport. We're able to quickly build it into tools that can help predict poaching and at the same time ensure that game wardens aren't at risk, or that can compare satellite and aerial imagery from before and after natural disasters in order to prioritize rescues and to reduce the risk of additional casualties.

There's so much modern AI can do, building different solutions out of the same common building blocks. Depending on the data you use to train the model, an image recognition algorithm can identify and count endangered snow leopards or tell the difference between contaminated beer and the scuffs on recycled and reused bottles.

AI can also add features to apps and workflows like recognizing speech, objects in photos, handwriting, or the fields on a paper form, or generating insights to go with data visualizations. It can automate routine work or even data analysis to free up the time of employees overwhelmed by the flood of information for the interesting, creative parts of their job—whether that's sales staff, customer support, or healthcare managers. It can even help with writing code, generating a complex data query, or filling in the rest of a commonly written function.

With modern machine learning tools, what were research projects with teams of computer scientists have become services you can use in your own applications, treating them as drop-in components. Or if you need more, using a common framework data scientists and business analysts can work together to fine-tune custom models and have them ready for use in just a few hours.

From Milestones to Models to Architectures

The Azure AI services we'll be covering in this book are based on decades of research at Microsoft that culminated in a series of breakthroughs over the last five years. In 2016, a Microsoft machine learning mode achieved parity with humans at identifying specific objects in photos and videos. In 2017, Microsoft speech recognition matched human transcription of telephone calls into text, and in 2018, a Microsoft machine learning system showed that it could read through documents and answer questions about the information in them at the same level as humans. In the same year, Microsoft reached the same benchmarks in synthesizing speech and translating between languages.

Those breakthroughs in speech recognition, translation, image classification, and text understanding were mostly built using supervised learning: taking large numbers of examples, labeling them carefully, and using them to train machine learning models to perform tasks like recognizing objects in images.

Around 2019, self-supervised learning techniques allowed researchers to take large corpora of content that hadn't been labeled—like the contents of public websites in many different languages—and have machine learning models map out the patterns of how words are used together, known as contextual semantics. That approach creates models that reach human levels of language understanding on tasks like summarizing documents or question and answer conversations between bots and humans: the models work by predicting which words should come next, deriving what people are trying to ask and retrieving the best answers.

The same approach powers analyzing and interpreting images and videos to retrieve the most relevant images, break a video up into segments, or describe objects in a scene when the model can recognize them but hasn't been specifically trained on how best to describe them. That way, you can generate captions about people holding accordions, bagpipes, or lutes without needing a training set that covers captions for every conceivable musical instrument someone could carry.

Over that time, the models to deliver these breakthroughs were also getting larger and more demanding: from 200 million to 2 billion parameters in 2018, 170 billion parameters in 2020, and 530 billion in 2021 for the Megatron-Turing Natural

Language Generation model. If the hardware can keep up and the costs don't get out of hand, machine learning models could keep growing, into trillions of parameters.

Alongside the new models, Microsoft also developed optimization techniques like DeepSpeed's Zero Redundancy Optimizer and other parallelism technologies that split the different parts of the models across data parallel processes,[1] and the ONNX Runtime that accelerates the basic building blocks of training deep learning models.

But even with all that optimization, these very large AI models are still very resource intensive, trained on huge clusters of hundreds of thousands of powerful GPUs and field-programmable gate arrays (FPGAs) interconnected by high-bandwidth networks, using a globally distributed scheduling service.[2] So Microsoft trains a small number of very large models and reuses them in lots of places, using transfer learning: transferring the general, foundational grammar and context skills gained with self-supervised learning to apply to specific domains. Those fine-tuned, pretrained models work with much smaller labeled datasets; in the future, that could be efficient enough to give every user their own personalized language model.

Azure also runs large models developed elsewhere: it's the only platform where OpenAI's groundbreaking GPT-3 large language models are available. Microsoft uses them to power GitHub's Copilot code writing feature and to turn natural language into Data Analysis Expressions (DAX) queries in Power Apps (see Chapter 6 for more about the Power Platform). In Dynamics 365, OpenAI offers suggestions for writing marketing content—even if what it suggests isn't perfect, it can offer more inspiration than staring at a blank page. Developers can use the language generation in their own applications by calling the OpenAI APIs through Cognitive Services, sending a request and maybe some examples in simple text and getting generated text back, ready to use. (We'll look at how to use the Azure OpenAI Service in Chapter 4.)

The platform that provides the massive scale needed for building those very large models, cross-training them to specific models, and running them in production is also what delivers the Azure AI services developers can use themselves—again, based on those very large models.

Azure AI services take away the burden of building and managing infrastructure for machine learning. They include the levels of scale, security, compliance, and governance that organizations expect from an enterprise-grade platform, like dedicated throughput, consistent latency, network isolation, managed identity, authentication, and guarantees backed by regulatory certifications (we'll look at this in detail in Chapter 8 as part of machine learning best practices).

---

1 The DeepSpeed optimization library is open source; find the repo and tutorials at DeepSpeed (*https://www.deepspeed.ai*).

2 See "Singularity: Planet-Scale, Preemptive and Elastic Scheduling of AI Workloads." (*https://arxiv.org/pdf/2202.07848.pdf*)

Cloud AI services can also help with delivering responsible AI, because if they're built to try and ensure that AI has a positive impact and to avoid unfairness and other issues, all the applications built with them can benefit from those principles because every developer doesn't have to solve the same problems on their own. That's always been one of the advantages of cloud services in general, although it's just a starting point, and in Chapter 8, we'll look at the tools, techniques, and responsible deployment choices you can use to build on that foundation.

The various Azure AI services can speed up training your own models using popular frameworks and powerful MLOps capabilities, simplify deployment (in the cloud, on mobile devices, and at the edge), provide pretrained models, or turn a machine learning problem into an API call. That means you can augment the familiar service-oriented architecture—where you scale IT by building services that communicate with each other—with AI-oriented architecture, where you have machine learning models and functions from AI services alongside the input and program logic that make up your app.

Just like you think about data schemas for your database, you need to think about datasets and labels. Experimentation becomes part of your development process the same way debugging already is. Telemetry from your application could feed back into your machine learning models, as well as telling you when you have a bug or giving you an idea for a new feature.

That makes for a more complex architecture (Figure 1-1 is an example of this for adding handwriting recognition to an app) and could mean a more complicated workflow. But the Azure AI services are designed to simplify that.

When you use the Cognitive Services we look at in Chapter 4, this kind of architecture is behind the APIs you call. You'll need to create your own equivalent with the building blocks in Azure Machine Learning if you're creating your own machine learning models: we'll walk you through that in Chapter 3. Whether you use your own models or call the ready-made services, the case studies in Chapters 10, 11, and 12 will give you some examples of how to integrate AI services into applications and architectures. And if you're wondering what the architecture that the cloud AI services run on looks like, we take a look at the Cognitive Services backend in Chapter 9.

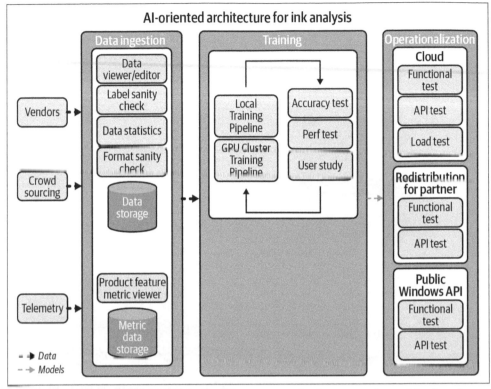

Figure 1-1. Adding handwriting recognition to your app from scratch would take a lot of work at every stage, from gathering data to training models to supporting them in production: Azure AI services can turn that into an SDK or an API you call

Ready to Jump In?

The potential of AI is enormous; the complexity of delivering that potential shouldn't be a burden for every developer and organization. In this chapter, we've looked at the research behind Azure AI and the promise of using cloud AI to add power to your apps and workflows without also adding complexity. That doesn't mean dumbing down development or restricting what tools and platforms you can use. In the next chapter, we'll show you just how broad the Azure AI platform is, before diving into how to use some of the specific services on offer.

## PART II

Tools and Services to Help You Build AI-Oriented Architectures

## CHAPTER 2

Understanding AI Offerings and Capabilities

You have a lot of options for building and using AI. In this chapter we're going to look at just how broad the Microsoft AI platform is, especially in the cloud. Many of these tools and services will be covered in detail later in the book, but we'll mention other possibilities as well to help you pick what fits your problem.

As AI techniques mature, so do the options for working with them. There's a shortage of data scientists and engineers; developing internal expertise in building and operating large-scale machine learning systems is expensive. With cloud AI services, there's no need for every organization to reimplement the same machine learning models when a cloud service can be trained to a high degree of accuracy and run at scale, offering access through well-defined APIs at very low cost to users.

These services simplify building custom models or integrating AI tools into existing workflows, bringing AI development within reach of domain experts and general business users. There are Azure AI options to suit a wide range of users with different levels of expertise and in a choice of different tools.

AI Services for All Types of Users

Machine learning now powers the Internet of Things (IoT), helps businesses analyze their present and predict their future, and assist consumers with everything from healthcare to gaming. Building AI into your applications and workflow is an option for an increasingly wide spectrum of users, too.

Popular frameworks make it easy to build and train custom machine learning models using deep neural networks, while cloud services like Azure offer pretrained models and customizable services that can quickly add machine learning functions to your applications with the minimum of code. These tools can help all users, from business analysts and information workers to developers:

Information workers

Business applications like Word and PowerPoint already use AI services to offer writing and design suggestions, transcribe meetings, and coach users on giving better presentations. Low-code and no-code tools that let users create their own custom workflows and apps include AI services that can enrich information and analyze data, like recognizing business cards or analyzing sentiment in customer feedback.

Business analysts

Modern business analysis techniques now require significant data science input. What used to be OLAP (online analytical processing) cubes and Excel spreadsheets are now big data exercises relying on complex models to find key trends and data points. Machine learning tools can help build and run those models, making AI an important tool for data science. By training a model or calling a pretrained model to enrich or find insights in your data, you can create predictions about future trends or emerging anomalies, allowing businesses to correct course quickly and avoid expensive problems. Developers and data scientists can also train custom models and make those available to users across the business in a curated catalog.

App developers

A significant role for machine learning is adding assistive technology to a wide range of apps. Using computer vision tools, we can make it easy to turn photographs into text, fill out forms, and manage personal data. Speech tools can add voice recognition, provide near real-time transcriptions and translations, or turn text into speech for first-line workers and others who can't conveniently look at a screen. Abled and disabled users can all take advantage of these technologies: the same tools can help provide hands-free control in cars or add voice controls to smart homes. Microsoft's AI for Good grants provide financial support for organizations that want to use AI tools and techniques for accessibility, using many of the services we cover in this book.

Industrial developers

The Internet of Things is a powerful source of data, from cameras and other complex edge devices to streams of data from connected sensors. With billions of connected devices, traditional algorithms struggle to pull relevant data out of the growing flood. Machine learning techniques can identify key data points, identifying errors and issues or predicting failure before it happens to ensure that systems continue to run safely with minimal downtime.

Where to Get Started on a Cloud Development Journey if You're New to This

The modern public cloud is a lot more than computers that someone else looks after. Building on hyperscale infrastructures, a cloud service delivers a global, distributed computing platform with access to vast amounts of compute and storage; far more than any individual organization could ever put in their own data centers. The economics of scale that allow cloud providers to run all their hardware mean anyone can tap into that compute capacity at prices that start at cents per hour.

Much of the cloud capacity is used for infrastructure, hosting virtual machines (VMs) that run software for customers or for cloud providers themselves. This infrastructure is also the foundation for platform services run and managed by cloud providers, with simple API access to bring them into your code. Platform services offer massive scale storage and databases, managed distributed computing environments, and much more.

Cloud APIs use familiar REST techniques to make services accessible from any development platform, in your choice of language. Using standard techniques makes them easy to build into everything from mobile applications to massive global-scale services, accessible from anywhere at any time. Things are even easier if you're using a popular language, with SDKs offering prebuilt libraries that wrap cloud to application communications in simple method calls.

In this book, we focus on Microsoft's various Azure machine learning tools, and you'll need an Azure account to use them. You can try out much of what we'll be looking at using a free Azure account or the developer resources that come with a Visual Studio subscription.

For new users, open the Azure home page (*http://azure.microsoft.com*) and click the "Try Azure for free" button. This gives you (at the time of writing) a $200 credit for a month and free access for 12 months to key Azure services, including the AI services, at Standard tiers. You can find a list of the available services (*https://azure.microsoft.com/en-us/free*).[1] Use a Microsoft account or a GitHub account to sign in and set up your Azure services: if you don't have one, you can create a new account using any email address as part of the sign-up process. Similarly, you can use free trials for Power Platform and other Microsoft 365 services.

If you already have an Azure account, you can try almost all of the services we write about in this book using the available free tiers (although some features may require additional pay-as-you-go services).

---

[1] If you're new to Azure, the Microsoft Learn course on Azure fundamentals (*https://go.microsoft.com/fwlink/?linkid=2190148*) will get you up to speed.

To help you get started quickly, check out the free Visual Studio Code editor, which has language support for .NET and for Python, including Jupyter Notebooks (commonly used to develop and test machine learning models and applications). There are Visual Studio Code extensions that let you use GitHub for source control and manage access to Azure tools, services, and resources directly from the editor. Azure also offers development tools in its portal that can help manage big data and build, train, and test your own machine learning models.

Microsoft's AI Offerings

Drawing on the expertise of Microsoft Research, Microsoft uses AI extensively in its own products and services for everything from predicting hardware failures in Azure data centers to designing custom slide layouts in PowerPoint and detecting previously unseen malware.

Through the Microsoft AI platform, those same AI techniques are available to data engineers who want to boost their productivity and take advantage of cloud scale, using cloud infrastructure and services or Microsoft frameworks and tools to build AI into applications on any infrastructure. Developers can use advanced machine learning algorithms through Azure cloud services that make it easy to operationalize them. And business analysts without AI expertise can use the same underlying services to gain advanced insights into data inside the Microsoft tools they're familiar with.

AI capabilities in familiar systems like SQL Server and low-code/no-code tools like the Power Platform bring the same models and algorithms to a wider range of users. The overlap between the various services and tools available as part of Microsoft's broad AI platform gives developers the choice of how they prefer to work. It also allows work done in one service to be reused through another. That could be running a cloud-trained machine learning model in a container for edge deployment or developers building custom machine learning models that business analysts can incorporate in reports.

This flexibility means there may be several options that could be appropriate for your specific project. As Figure 2-1 shows, developers might use a managed service to build their own AI models or take advantage of cloud infrastructure services to scale machine learning models created with open source frameworks. They can use those models to build on the extensible AI in a business platform, take advantage of AI tools in familiar infrastructure products and operating systems, or simply call prebuilt but customizable AI APIs.

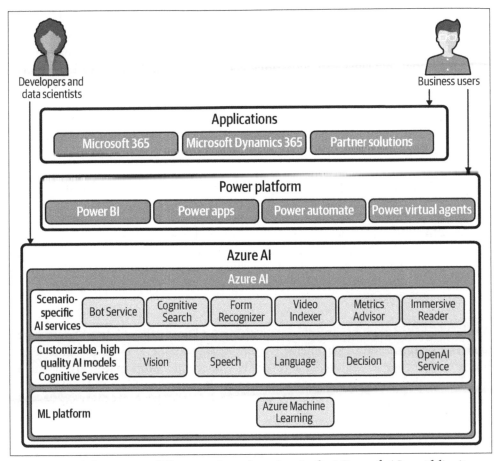

Figure 2-1. With so many different tools and services in the Microsoft AI portfolio, it helps to look at who the services are designed for as well as what they offer

Managed AI Services and Infrastructure Options in Azure

Azure Machine Learning is a managed cloud service aimed at accelerating and managing the data science lifecycle, where you can use pretrained models or train, deploy, and manage your own models in the cloud or to edge devices. Developers who prefer to work in a command-line interface (CLI) can use Python, R, and Jupyter Notebooks, taking advantage of open source frameworks like PyTorch, TensorFlow, and scikit-learn, and automating the machine learning lifecycle with GitHub and Azure Pipelines.

You can also work with Azure Machine Learning through SDKs or the Azure Machine Learning studio web interface, which supports both code-first and low-code development. There's a drag-and-drop designer to train and deploy machine learning models through pipelines without writing code, a graphical UI for creating automated machine learning experiments and integration with managed Jupyter Notebook servers. For deployment, models can be converted to ONNX, run as web services (using containers in the cloud or locally) using CPU, GPU, or FPGA infrastructure for inferencing, shared with Power BI for use in data analytics or deployed directly to Azure IoT Edge devices.

 Azure Machine Learning studio is a different service from the older ML Studio, a standalone visual design tool for building machine learning models by connecting datasets to preconfigured algorithms and modules; once deployed, the models are published as web services. Although it's still available, ML Studio isn't as powerful or flexible as the visual design tools integrated into Azure Machine Learning, and existing users will want to consider migrating.

Azure Machine Learning can integrate with Azure Databricks, a hosted Spark-based analytics platform with rich interactive workspaces for developing machine learning models in collaboration with other developers; the workspaces are based on Notebooks that can contain runnable Python, R, Scala, or SQL code, along with visualizations, instructions, and explanations. Azure Databricks is ideal for running large-scale intensive machine learning workflows that use open source machine learning libraries and MLflow for automation.

Organizations that have adopted Azure Arc, Microsoft's software solution for managing on-premises, hybrid, and multi-cloud infrastructure through Azure Resource Manager, can use it to run a selection of Azure services in any Kubernetes environment. Arc-enabled data services allow you to run Azure SQL Managed Instance and Azure PostgreSQL Hyperscale on Arc-managed Kubernetes infrastructure, and one of the main reasons organizations want to run those cloud database services on their own infrastructure is for machine learning. In preview at the time of writing, Azure Arc-enabled Machine Learning allows you to run Azure Machine Learning as a cloud service on your own infrastructure to work with data stored in those database services.

Machine learning and data experts who don't need a managed machine learning service but want to work with a powerful set of data science tools without needing to spend time on installation, configuration, and getting all the dependencies right can save time with the Azure Data Science VMs. These prebuilt images for Windows or Linux come with Microsoft and open source data science and development tools preinstalled and ready to use, on CPU or GPU-accelerated VMs.

Business Platforms with Extensible AI

Not every organization can invest in a team of data scientists or machine learning developers, and you don't need development expertise to add AI features to your workflow. Cloud services allow organizations to take advantage of the latest break-throughs using components that require little or no coding. Extensible machine learning is integrated into Microsoft's low-code, no-code, and automation platforms like Power BI, Power Apps, and Logic Apps.

The Power BI cloud service includes a data preparation workflow that can use auto-mated machine learning from Azure Machine Learning to allow business analysts to train, validate, and call binary prediction, classification, and regression models to analyze their data. Power BI automatically finds the most relevant features to include in the model, selects the right algorithm, and tunes the model, generating a report that explains what fields in the data influence the predictions and how well the model will perform.

The AI Builder feature in Power Apps and Power Automate lets you use prebuilt models that can do things like translate text, process receipts (even handwritten ones), or recognize contact information from business cards in a wizard-like expe-rience. But you can also use machine learning models provided by developers in your organization or train your own models for detecting objects, processing forms, extracting entity information, and making predictions or classifications.

If you want more details on the AI features you can use in the different services in the Microsoft Power Platform or with Logic Apps, turn to Chapter 6.

AI for Big Data and Relational Data

Although we don't have space to cover these in detail, there are options for building and using AI in an increasing number of products and platforms that developers and users are already using. Databases and analytics platforms are obvious places to do machine learning: running machine learning models where the data resides delivers the lowest latency and highest performance because the data doesn't have to move around. Operating systems and application frameworks are also starting to include libraries to accelerate machine learning inferencing in native applications:

- SQL Server Machine Learning Services puts an analytics engine that supports R and Python libraries inside SQL Server so developers can use machine learning like any other database functions they're writing. If you've adopted SQL Server Big Data Clusters, Machine Learning Services on SQL Server Big Data Clusters run Python and R scripts on the master instance.

Although those are both server products, you can run them in Azure VMs for scale—or use the Azure equivalent, Machine Learning Services in Azure SQL Managed Instance, to run Python and R scripts for predictive analytics and machine learning using stored procedures or T-SQL.

- If you use Azure Data Studio for editing and running SQL queries, the Machine Learning extension (in preview at the time of writing), lets you import machine learning models, make predictions, and create notebooks to run experiments with data in SQL databases.

- The Azure Synapse Analytics cloud service combines enterprise data warehousing and big data analytics; that includes training machine learning models with SparkML, MLib, and other libraries like scikit-learn, but there's integration between Azure Synapse Notebooks and Azure Machine Learning. You can run batch scoring with models whether they were trained in Azure Synapse or outside it.

- Suppose you don't need the Azure Machine Learning integration of Azure Databricks or Synapse. In that case, Azure HDInsight is an open source cloud analytics service that includes Microsoft's implementation of Apache Spark and MMLSpark, Microsoft's machine learning library for Spark, which can process data in Azure Storage and Azure Data Lake.

Making Machine Learning More Portable

The Open Neural Network Exchange (ONNX) standard for representing machine learning models in a portable format simplifies optimizing models for inferencing across multiple platforms. You can convert models from common frameworks to ONNX to take advantage of accelerators on different hardware platforms, without needing to rewrite the model to optimize it for each one. The ONNX Runtime also offers performance gains for inferencing on CPU without additional hardware accelerators.

The Azure Custom Vision service generates ONNX models. You can train and deploy ONNX models in Azure Machine Learning, creating cloud-hosted REST endpoints that can be consumed like any other API (we cover this in detail in the next chapter), or use them to make predictions from data in Azure SQL Edge and Azure SQL Managed Instance.

ONNX models can also be used by machine learning frameworks, even if they're not the ones the model was trained in. That means they can run inside Windows applications using the Windows ML (WinML) inference engine in Windows 10, Windows Server 2019, and later releases, using the GPU for performance.

ML.NET is a cross-platform open source machine learning framework for integrating custom machine learning models (including ONNX models) that perform tasks like sentiment analysis, product recommendation, value prediction, fraud detection, or image classification into .NET applications. You can build, train, and deploy custom models with the graphical ML.NET Model Builder Visual Studio extension; this uses automated machine learning to find the best algorithm for your model and generates the code to add the ML.NET model to your .NET application.

The cross-platform ML.NET CLI can generate the model and C# code to run it, but for a smaller number of scenarios than the Visual Studio extension.

Infer.NET is another open source .NET library for machine learning, this time for probabilistic inference, using a statistical model that makes it easy to interpret results and learn as new data arrives. It's used in the Halo TrueSkill ranking service that finds gamers a suitable opponent, and it also powers the service in Azure Machine Learning that suggests which machine learning algorithm to use with your data.

Cognitive Services

For developers who want more control over how they use AI tools but who don't want to become experts in building and running machine learning systems, Azure Cognitive Services offers prebuilt machine learning services you can call from inside your code or run on your own servers and in devices at the edge of the network. Make a call to a REST API or work with an SDK, and you can instantly start using powerful machine learning models for Vision, Speech, Language, Decisions, and Search without needing expertise in data science.

Designed to be easy to use at global scale, in a single app, or running a model locally in a container, and to be economical because you pay by usage, Cognitive Services make it possible for you to take advantage of the latest breakthroughs in AI without building and deploying your own models.

If you're building your own machine learning systems, operationalizing them to use in production at scale can take as long as—or longer than—developing the right machine learning models to generate the insights you want in the first place. The data used to train and run machine learning models can be very personal, or critical to your business, so you need to deploy the infrastructure for those systems with strong security. And you need to keep them up to date as new techniques are developed, retrain them regularly to make sure the models continue to perform well as the data they work with changes over time, or build out new systems to keep up with the different ways your users want to work.

Cognitive Services takes away the majority of that work, and it gives you global cloud scale with options for the edge. You don't have to train the models used in Cognitive Services; Microsoft delivers pretrained models as services and regularly updates them with improved training sets to ensure that they stay relevant and can work with as wide a range of source materials as possible. New and improved algorithms and models are regularly added to the different services; in some cases, your app will get more powerful without you needing to make any changes.

They run in more than 30 Azure regions around the world, with data stored and retained in compliant ways that help address responsible AI and the other best practices we look at in Chapters 7 and 8. Services are localized into multiple languages, with some services available in over 100 languages. Speech-to-text, for example, is available in 30 languages and complies with ISO, SOC, and HIPAA standards. They offer strict service level agreements (SLAs) and are guaranteed to be available at least 99.9% of the time. But you can also take some of the most useful Cognitive Services and run them locally in containers if latency or regulations require it, or export a model and build it into an app.

Even though they're delivered as cloud services that can be called in a few lines of code, some specific Cognitive Services allow you to customize the data model to get better results for your particular problem:

- You can create a custom vision model that has the power of image recognition trained on millions of images and quickly retrain it to recognize specific people, objects, or places—the products you make or sell, or whether a retail store is following rules about how to display items and promotions or how many people are allowed in at once.

- You can teach the Conversational Language Understanding Service jargon, slang, regional colloquialisms, and all the other details of phrasing that often confuse automated systems.

- You can model the acoustics of the shopping mall or racetrack where your app is going to be used, so speech recognition is more accurate.

- You can create custom voices so generated speech for a phone service, AI assistant, or any other text-to-speech scenario doesn't only sound natural, it sounds like the kind of voice you want to have speaking for your brand and your organization—or even the celebrity associated with your brand, whether that's a real person or Bugs Bunny.

As cloud services, Cognitive Services are continually improving and being added to. For example, Cognitive Research Technologies includes experimental APIs and SDKs that are still in development in the Cognitive Services Labs. These aren't production-grade Azure services: they're free "as is" previews for getting an early look at brand-new areas that might or might not graduate to full-fledged services.

Other AI services also build on or work with Cognitive Services, like the low-code options we cover in Chapter 6.

Azure Applied AI Services combine multiple Cognitive Services with models and business logic ready to use for specific tasks, often with a dedicated portal that lets business users as well as developers contribute. The built-in AI enrichment skills in the Azure Cognitive Search service for unstructured content and content that is unsearchable in its raw form—like scanned documents, complex PDFs, blobs, or text that needs to be translated—are based on pretrained machine learning models in the vision and text analytics Cognitive Services APIs.

Azure Bot Service is a managed bot development environment for building enterprise conversational AI using templates and the Microsoft Bot Framework.

If you want to jump in to working with Azure Cognitive Services and Applied AI Services, turn straight to Chapter 4.

How to Determine What Tool Is Best for You

With many different options for building machine learning systems, choosing the right one for your applications can be confusing, especially as you can achieve similar results from different tools and services. One way is to think about how you want to work with machine learning—through code or a visual interface—and how much flexibility you want. Figure 2-2 shows how different Microsoft AI options fit into that spectrum.

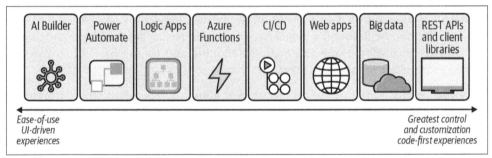

Figure 2-2. Different options for working with Microsoft's cloud AI services fall on a spectrum from no code to pro code, with more options for customizing as you invest more in coding

It can also help to start by thinking about the possible constraints, whether that's where the training data is stored, where the live data will need to be processed, or your own skills and preferences.

Microsoft's machine learning tools can be used on premises, in hybrid systems, or in the cloud. You can use prebuilt APIs from Cognitive Services or build your own using the Azure Machine Learning service, running models in the cloud or on your own hardware—both in data centers and on the edge of the network.

Azure offers a range of different tools for different needs and for different levels of expertise. If you want prebuilt models with limited customization that can be accessed through APIs and used in traditional or low-code development, Azure Cognitive Services has APIs for Vision, Speech, Language, Search, and Decision support. All you need to is pick an API, choose an SDK, and start writing code to use it. Simple web-based training tools allow you to customize models using your own data for a number of the services.

There's also support for the Cognitive Services APIs in Microsoft's low-code Power Platform, in tools like the Power BI analytics platform and in both Power Apps and Power Automate. Making basic machine learning plug and play allows anyone who can build an Excel spreadsheet to use AI in their own personal applications and workflows.

If you prefer to build your own models, you can use the Azure Machine Learning service to build, train, and test them. Python has rapidly become an important tool for machine learning specialists, but while your choice of development language will have an impact on the techniques and tools you use, there are still multiple options.

The hosted Notebook service in Azure Machine Learning where you can build and test models using a selection of popular machine learning frameworks is based on its Python SDK. If you prefer local development, the SDK is available along with Visual Studio Code extensions to develop and run code for most machine learning frameworks on your own PCs using locally hosted Jupyter Notebooks. But if you don't use Python or R, there's a visual development interface for building models and a form-like AutoML tool for automatically training and tuning models, so you can still take advantage of the cloud service.

How you deploy a machine learning system is going to depend on where workloads need to be deployed, how much data you will be processing, and what type of actionable responses you need from a system. Can the data for inferencing be kept on premises, or will you need to take advantage of Azure's big data services and flexible compute?

Networks remain a key constraint on any machine learning system. While models can be relatively small, you are likely to be moving significant amounts of data. You will need to consider both bandwidth and latency; are your applications sharing a limited network connection with other applications? Is there a requirement for a response from a model within a specific time?

Models running in the Azure Machine Learning service can be accessed through REST APIs, or they can be exported as ONNX for use elsewhere, from mobile devices to other cloud platforms.

If inferencing is going to run on the device, you can use Windows' built-in machine learning tooling using its WinML APIs, which can accelerate ONNX models. Using Azure for development and training takes advantage of its flexible CPU and memory options, allowing you to spin up a development environment as needed and then disposing of it when it's no longer needed. There's no need to invest in high-performance training and development systems; all you need to run are your own inferencing environments.

Applications running on the edge are likely to need to work with tooling running in local containers. The range of Azure Stack hardware provides a container host that can use Cognitive Services locally while still managing them through the Azure portal. Local compute can also take advantage of AI accelerators like Intel's Movidius computer vision module or using GPU compute on modern GPUs.

Cognitive Services containers are also useful when working with IoT solutions. By running a local Azure IoT Hub instance with the appropriate Cognitive Services container, you can process data streams from edge devices before delivering data to applications running in the cloud.

Sometimes the choice will come down to which data source you need to connect to. AI Builder needs data to be stored in Dataverse through the Power Platform; Logic Apps offers a similar low-code/no-code experience to Power Apps and can integrate with Azure Machine Learning and allows you to work with data from a wider range of sources. Newer services like the Azure Percept camera and audio edge platform use cloud no-code development tools to build and train vision models, which can then can be deployed to devices and used to deliver annotated streams of data for use in your applications.

Microsoft's AI tools and platforms are designed to work for all skill levels, from low-code development of predictive systems for business analysis to complex computer vision applications in cars and drones. You can choose the tool you want based on what you want to do, and then run it where you want. In this chapter, we've tried to give you an overview of the breadth of the Microsoft AI portfolio, with a handy summary in Table 2-1.

Table 2-1. Azure Machine Learning options at a glance

	Target user	What you can do with it	Graphical UI?	Subscriptions needed	For more details, see...
Cognitive Services	Developers, data scientists	Work with some Cognitive Services through a web portal or call any service from any language and environment	Code-only client libraries and REST APIs; some services include a web portal for setup/testing	Azure account + Cognitive Services resources	Chapter 4

	Target user	What you can do with it	Graphical UI?	Subscriptions needed	For more details, see...
Azure Cognitive Services for Big Data	Developers, data engineers	Use data in Apache Spark services like Azure Databricks, Azure Synapse, Azure Kubernetes Service, and Data Connectors with Cognitive Services	Code only	Azure account + Cognitive Services resources	Chapter 4 and "Azure Cognitive Services for Big Data" (*https://oreil.ly/d8jgP*)
Azure Functions and Azure Service Web Jobs	Developers, data scientists	Call Cognitive Services APIs and client libraries from serverless event-driven code	Yes	Azure account + Cognitive Services resource + Azure Functions subscription	Chapter 4
Azure Applied AI Services	Developers, business users	Use multiple Cognitive Services with task-specific models, sometimes through a GUI with domain-specific business logic; extend with your own Azure Machine Learning models	Yes	Azure account + Cognitive Services resources	Chapter 5
Azure Logic Apps	Developers, integrators, IT pros, DevOps	Call Cognitive Services through service-specific connectors that wrap the APIs from low-code apps with integrations to business data sources	Yes	Azure account + Cognitive Services resource + Logic Apps deployment	Chapter 6
Azure DevOps and GitHub Actions	Developers, data scientists, data engineers	Use continuous integration/ continuous deployment (CI/CD) to call Cognitive Services APIs; to train, update, test, and deploy custom Cognitive Services Language Understanding and Speech models; or to build an Azure Machine Learning pipeline	Code only	Azure account + GitHub account (Cognitive Services resources or Azure Machine Learning as required)	Chapter 8 and Language Understanding Service (LUIS) (*https://oreil.ly/O0bhe*), speech (*https://oreil.ly/alijM*), and Azure Machine Learning (*https://oreil.ly/ilL3B*)
Power Apps	Developers, business users	Call Cognitive Services in low-code apps using service-specific connectors that wrap the APIs or use prebuilt and custom models that encapsulate some Cognitive Services	Yes	Azure account + Cognitive Services resource + Power Apps subscription	Chapter 6

	Target user	What you can do with it	Graphical UI?	Subscriptions needed	For more details, see...
Power Automate	Business users and SharePoint administrators	Call Cognitive Services through service-specific connectors that wrap the APIs from low-code automation workflows	UI only	Azure account + Cognitive Services resource + Power Automate subscription + Office 365 subscription	Chapter 6
AI Builder	Business users, analysts, and SharePoint administrators	Use prebuilt and custom models that encapsulate some Cognitive Services in Power Apps, Power Automate, or Dynamics 365	UI only	Power Apps, Power Automate, or Dynamics 365 subscription + AI Builder add-on	Chapter 6
Power BI	Business users, data engineers	Import and clean data to visualize in reports that use AI to offer insights; call custom or prebuilt machine learning models; prepare data for training machine learning models	Yes	Power BI subscription	Chapter 6
Azure Machine Learning	Data scientists, data engineers, developers	Build, train, deploy, and serve models in the cloud (or to run at the edge) using MLOps/DevOps and a wide range of algorithms and frameworks	Yes	Azure account (VM pricing plus Azure Blob storage, Azure Key Vault, Azure Container Registry, Application Insights, and other services as required)	Chapter 3
Azure Arc-enabled Machine Learning	Developers, data scientists, data engineers, IT pros, DevOps	Build and train models using Azure Machine Learning on your own Kubernetes infrastructure managed through Azure Arc	Yes	Azure account (Azure Policy, other Azure and Azure Arc-enabled services as required)	"Run Azure Machine Learning Anywhere" (*https://oreil.ly/ LM3as*)
Azure Synapse Analytics	IT pros, SharePoint administrators, developers, data scientists, data engineers	Ingest, prepare, explore, and serve data for machine learning without ETL	Yes	Azure account + Azure Synapse Analytics	"Machine Learning Capabilities in Azure Synapse Analytics" (*https://oreil.ly/ VFhuq*)

	Target user	What you can do with it	Graphical UI?	Subscriptions needed	For more details, see...
Azure HDInsight	Data scientists, data engineers	Use SparkML, MLib, and MMLSpark to build models on data stored in Apache Hadoop, Spark, Hive, or Kafka; use Hive queries for feature engineering for Azure Machine Learning models	Yes	Azure account + Azure HDInsight	"Machine Learning on HDInsight" (*https://oreil.ly/nv3pl*)
Azure Databricks Machine Learning	Data scientists, data engineers	Train, manage, deploy, and serve machine learning models using MLflow or Azure Machine Learning	UI only	Azure account + Azure Databricks	"Databricks Machine Learning guide" (*https://oreil.ly/IvyDl*)
SQL Server Machine Learning Services	Database admins, data scientists, data engineers	Run Python and R scripts, packages, and frameworks like PyTorch, TensorFlow, and scikit-learn against relational data for machine learning	Yes	SQL Server 2017 and later or Azure account + Azure SQL Managed Instance	SQL ML overview (*https://oreil.ly/Jhghm*)
Machine Learning Services on SQL Server Big Data Clusters	Database admins, data scientists, data engineers	Run Python and R scripts using Spark, MLib, and H2O AutoML to select and tune models on data in Hadoop Distributed File System storage pools in containers on Kubernetes	Yes	SQL Server 2019 and later + Kubernetes infrastructure such as Azure Kubernetes Service	SQL Server Big Data Clusters (*https://oreil.ly/gileg*)
Azure Data Studio Machine Learning extension	Database admins, data scientists, data engineers	Import models, make predictions, or use notebooks with SQL databases from the Azure Data Studio IDE	Yes	SQL Server with SQL Server Machine Learning Services	"Machine Learning extension for Azure Data Studio" (*https://oreil.ly/MfVYf*)

We can't cover all those options in this book, and there are other O'Reilly titles that tackle several of them in depth. But in the next chapters, we'll show you how to use the Microsoft AI services that leverage the cloud to offer you both flexibility and scale. Let's start with Azure Machine Learning, the cloud service where you can build and train your own machine learning models to call from the cloud or build into containers to run locally.

## CHAPTER 3

Train, Tune, and Deploy Models with Azure Machine Learning, ONNX, and PyTorch

In the previous chapter, we tried to cover the full range of AI tools and services available from Microsoft. Now let's focus on how you can use the Azure Machine Learning cloud service to build and train your own models, using familiar machine learning frameworks and a mix of Azure and Visual Studio tooling. We'll be looking at how you can use the popular PyTorch machine learning framework as well as how you can export trained models as ONNX for use with local inferencing runtimes, like ML.Net.

Understanding Azure Machine Learning

Microsoft's approach to machine learning is to target different products to different groups of users, with different skill levels and different expectations for the technologies they're using. At one end of the scale is the Power Platform's AI Builder's task-focused low-code connectors (we'll look at those in Chapter 6), while at the other is Azure Machine Learning. Designed for experienced data scientists, it provides a cloud-based development environment where you can design, train, run, and manage machine learning models using popular frameworks.

The Azure Machine Learning environment is best thought of as a set of tools that all address the same backend model hosting infrastructure but that can be mixed and matched to fit with the way you want to work. If you're new to advanced machine learning development, you can work with a drag-and-drop designer to build models, much like a low-code development environment. Experienced data scientists can use the numerical methods language R to build and test models, working with R's own development tools through an Azure SDK. Meanwhile, Python machine learning developers can work with Jupyter Notebooks in Visual Studio Code or any other Python development environment.

Under the hood, Azure Machine Learning is a flexible environment that supports multiple machine learning frameworks and methodologies. That means support for popular open frameworks like PyTorch and TensorFlow, and the ability to export trained models in ONNX for use anywhere there's a compatible runtime. There's even a command line option, using the Azure CLI to manage your models.

We introduced ONNX in Chapter 2. Open Neural Network Exchange is a standard for representing machine learning models in a portable format that simplifies optimizing models for inferencing across multiple platforms. Models from common frameworks like TensorFlow, PyTorch, scikit-learn, Keras, Chainer, MXNet, MATLAB, and SparkML can be converted to ONNX to take advantage of accelerators on different hardware platforms (like TensorRT on NVidia GPUs, OpenVINO on Intel processors, or DirectML on Windows) when you want to operationalize them, without needing to rewrite the model to optimize it for each one.

It's a system that's designed to scale with you, from building and training models on local machines, to working with the cloud and with Azure data sources and compute. As you learn more and try new techniques, you're able to take the tools you're using and bring them to Azure, before delivering a machine learning model as a managed endpoint or an ONNX export. Once your model is trained, Azure Machine Learning makes it ready to run in your applications wherever they are, from mobile devices with neural processors to working with terabytes of data of all types stored in Azure Data Lakes or with streamed data from Event Grid and Azure IoT.

Understanding Azure Machine Learning Studio

Azure Machine Learning studio is a web portal-based model development and training tool designed for data scientists. As it's intended for different levels of experience and programming skill, it mixes traditional programming tools with no-code tools.

You shouldn't confuse it with the now deprecated ML Studio visual tooling. You still get the same visual design experience, but there's now full integration with the Azure Machine Learning SDKs, as well as more powerful model design and development tools. If anything, Azure Machine Learning is a significant upgrade, and any projects that still rely on ML Studio should be migrated to Azure Machine Learning. Models developed in the studio can be modified by developers using the SDK, while the studio tools can help tune models that have been developed using Python or R.

Microsoft recommends using the latest web browser releases to work with the Azure Machine Learning studio. Much of the studio editing experience relies on modern web technologies, building on the same Monaco code editing tools that are used by Visual Studio Code.

Developers of all types are catered for by Azure Machine Learning studio. Experienced Python data science developers can work in Jupyter Notebooks, using a live code development environment with real-time code evaluation and debugging, so you can see the effects of your code as you write it. Alternatively, you can start with existing models and datasets in the Azure Machine Learning designer, which gives you a drag-and-drop surface where you can build a machine learning pipeline from your datasets and Azure Machine Learning modules.

An alternate approach offers automated machine learning, where Azure Machine Learning fits and tunes a model to your data. You can use this in conjunction with the Azure Machine Learning data labeling service, which helps you prepare data for use in a machine learning model, adding appropriate labels to improve training. This set of options is very important for opening up machine learning to a wider audience. There's no need to have any data science experience, as you are guided through the process of uploading data and then selecting the best model for your data, finally testing it on more of your data to ensure that the resulting model is ready for use.

You can treat Azure Machine Learning studio as a one-stop shop for machine learning. It's where you can build and manage models, work with datasets, and add new data sources and storage. Other tools manage the compute resources used to build, test, and run models. Data science specialists get access to notebooks to build, run, and share experiments, with logs to help analyze results. At the same time, you can construct pipelines that bring data processing and machine learning together, ensuring that you have the best model for your problem.

Getting Started with Azure Machine Learning

Azure Machine Learning offers a mix of visual and code-based development tooling. In this section, we will look at how to configure and use its machine learning environments.

Setting Up a Machine Learning Environment

The Azure Machine Learning service is part of the Azure portal and managed like any other Azure resource. From the home screen, choose to add a new resource to your tenant, and pick "Machine learning." You'll recognize it by its icon, a mashup of the Azure logo with a glass experimental flask to signify its data science roots.

If you've not created any machine learning workspaces, click the Create button to start setting up your first workspace. This is where you work with data to build and test machine learning models. The process requires setting up additional Azure services to support your machine learning development and to host and share your trained models. Start by assigning your workspace to a subscription and a resource group. If you're just investigating the service, use a free trial account or credits from a Visual Studio or an Azure student account.

From the portal, set a name for your workspace and assign it to an Azure region. This will automatically create a new storage account, along with a key vault for credentials, and an application insights instance for debugging. There's also the option of choosing a container registry if you're planning on exporting models as containers for use outside of Azure.

Once you've completed the first page of settings, you're given the option of setting public or private endpoint details. A private endpoint is much more secure, but it does require configuring an Azure virtual network and a link to a private DNS; you'll need to work with your network team on this (and you may want to discuss the best practices for security and data access in Chapter 8 with them). While you're just experimenting with the service, a public endpoint should be sufficient.

The service's advanced settings give you the tools to manage account access, data encryption, and whether or not you're working with sensitive data. This last point is particularly important; as if your data contains personally identifiable information or commercially sensitive data you can choose to use a high business impact workspace. This reduces the diagnostic information sent to Microsoft as well as applying a higher standard of encryption.

Finally, you can apply tags to your workspace to help track its costs in your organization's billing statement. This is particularly important if you're sharing costs across business groups and where you may have multiple machine learning workspaces at any one time. You can then review your settings before creating your workspace. Usefully, Azure gives you the option of downloading an ARM template of your settings, so you can automate future deployments.

Click Create to build a workspace. This may take some time to deploy.

Once your workspace is deployed, you can launch Machine Learning studio to start work with your models. You'll find a URL for your studio workspace in the portal overview; bookmark this for quick access to the service in the future. It's also worth saving your workspace's properties, as these can be used by external tools to access Machine Learning services directly.

You may need to log in to the Machine Learning studio portal again using your Azure account; this runs as a specialized environment. Once logged in, you'll be presented with a welcome screen where you can choose different options to get started with building and training a model. The three most popular options get their own launch buttons, one for using Python and the machine learning SDK in a Notebook, one for using automated machine learning, and one for the machine learning.

The Machine Learning studio portal has three roles, detailed in the left-hand menu pane. These are Author, Assets, and Manage. Author gives access to the three key development environments, while Assets allows you to manage the features used to build and deliver machine learning services, from your datasets through experiments and pipelines, to your models and the endpoints used to access them. Finally, the Manage section helps you control Azure resources used by the studio, choosing the right compute and storage services.

There are other ways to set up an Azure Machine Learning environment. One option is to use the Azure Machine Learning Python SDK to set one up from your Python development environment, while another is to use the Azure CLI. Details of how to do this are in the platform documentation.

You can now start to build your Azure-hosted machine learning models.

Integration with Azure Services

An Azure Machine Learning workspace is a set of Azure resources, all bundled together using a common UI. Under the hood there's a set of VMs for handling compute, a storage account for your data, and integrations with Application Insights, Key Vault, and the Container Registry.

There's also support for Azure Active Directory (Azure AD), giving you role-based access control (RBAC). This can help manage user access to the service, controlling who gets to do what. For example, you can ensure that only data science team members get access to the storage accounts used to manage data.

It's worth using the guided experience tool to set up your first training environment, so you can see what resources you need to configure and how they need to be configured. Start by creating a compute environment. There are three options: an Azure Machine Learning compute cluster, an Azure Machine Learning compute instance, and using Kubernetes via Azure Arc. The Kubernetes option is an interesting one, as it allows you to set up your own machine learning cluster on your own hardware in your own data center.

If you're using Azure-hosted compute, pick the VM types you want to use as a host. You will be charged per VM instance per hour.

Compute VMs are available as general purpose, compute optimized, or memory optimized:

- Memory optimized VMs are best for training on large datasets, while compute optimized are best where latency is an issue.
- You can save money by choosing a low-priority VM, which may be preempted by other tasks. However, it's a trade-off that's worth making for experimentation.
- Other options allow you to choose to use a GPU VM, with your code automatically optimized for use on GPUs.

Select the option you want to use, and then choose a name and the number of nodes you intend to use, both minimum and maximum. You can also enable Secure Shell (SSH) access and connect your VM to a virtual network.

Wait for your compute instance to be created before continuing to set up your development environment. Once it's been created, you can select it and set up your machine learning platform. Azure Machine Learning studio provides four different models as Ubuntu-based VM images. You can choose between scikit-learn (with two options, one of which adds LightGBM and XGBoost support, which both can help speed up training), PyTorch, and TensorFlow. All four images are preconfigured with the Azure Machine Learning SDK and have the appropriate Python packages installed.

You can now configure your training job, setting up experiments and uploading your own code. Code will need a shell command to run from the upload directory, so be sure to add appropriate parameters and any necessary environment variables. Code can also be run from your workspace's Blob storage. At the same time, you'll need to configure your dataset, giving it a name and ensuring it's ready for use.

With everything in place, you're ready to run your first machine learning experiment using your Azure resources.

Using Visual Studio Code

You don't need to be logged into the Azure portal to use Azure Machine Learning. Microsoft provides a set of extensions for its Visual Studio Code editor (*https:// go.microsoft.com/fwlink/?linkid=2190261*) that add support to its suite of Azure tools.

Once installed from the Visual Studio Marketplace, the extension adds Machine Learning controls to its Azure control pane, alongside the other Azure extensions. Having all the Azure features in one place simplifies finding what you need, especially as you'll often be using different Azure features in the same applications. The extension simplifies working with Python-based machine learning products, and it's well worth installing the Visual Studio Code's Python language support in advance for

IntelliSense code completion, language server-based syntax highlighting, and linting, as well as built-in Jupyter Notebooks.

Next, sign into the extension with your Azure account to get access to your Azure Machine Learning resources. You can set a default workspace that gives you access to diagnostics and autocompletion, using the Azure Machine Learning commands that are added to the Visual Studio Code command palette by the extension. You can quickly create new resources as well as manage resources created through the portal, using Code to edit JavaScript Object Notation (JSON) schema. Once set up, resources can be started and stopped as needed.

It's worth ensuring you have Code's YAML and JSON tooling installed to help with managing Azure Machine Learning configurations.

Working with Azure Machine Learning resources inside your development environment simplifies and streamlines the process. You don't need to switch context; the same command palette you use for working with Python or with JavaScript APIs controls your Azure Machine Learning environment.

The same YAML editing environment is used to create training jobs, uploading local Python files to your choice of CPU or GPU compute clusters. Again, you'll need to choose an appropriate environment from Microsoft's library of curated images (*https://go.microsoft.com/fwlink/?linkid=2190139*).

The Azure Machine Learning Python SDK for Local Development

While Azure Machine Learning studio provides an environment for building and training models, experienced AI developers and data scientists may prefer to use familiar development environments and tools, bringing their own algorithms and numerical methods to Azure. One way to do this is using the Azure Machine Learning SDK for Python, along with your choice of Python development environments.

This allows you to install the SDK into a tool like Visual Studio Code and build and test your models from the Python command line or use Jupyter Notebooks on your own system to build, test, and share models using the notebook as an interactive test bed for code. Once installed, the SDK adds tools for working with the development lifecycle of models and datasets, as well as managing Azure cloud resources. You can then train models either in the cloud or on your own system, a useful option if you've got a significant amount of GPU processing capability.

While most users will prefer to use the SDK to train their models interactively, there's an option to use automated machine learning to tune models to find the best fit for your dataset. If you're a data scientist, you may well find this a useful way of delivering machine learning models from your data. Finally, the SDK provides tools to go from a model to an Azure-hosted REST API that can be called from any code.

The SDK provides a mix of stable production-ready features alongside experimental code. In practice you're likely to use the stable features, leaving the experiments for future exploration as they get closer to release, especially as they may well have bugs.

Much of the Azure Machine Learning platform is accessible through a series of classes in the SDK. These include foundational classes like Workspace, which creates workspace objects using your Azure subscription details. If you're planning on working with multiple models, save your configuration details as a JSON file, which can be called each time you create a new workspace.

Once you have a workspace, you'll need to create an Experiment to host your model runs and results. Runs are another class in their own right, creating a Run object that monitors a trial, with function calls to retrieve its results.

Install the SDK using pip:

```
pip install azure-ml core
```

Once it's installed, use an import statement to bring azureml.core into your runtime environment. This then allows you to create a workspace from code:

```
from azureml.core import Workspace
ws = Workspace.create(name='myworkspace',
                      subscription_id='<azure-subscription-id>',
                      resource_group='myresourcegroup',
                      create_resource_group=True,
                      location='eastus2'
                      )
```

If you're using the same account details for multiple scripts, save the configuration as a JSON file and load it for every script.

The following code snippet loads a configuration for a workspace, then opens an experiment, before running the experiment:

```
from azureml.core import Workspace, Experiment, Environment, ScriptRunConfig

ws = Workspace.from_config()
experiment = Experiment(workspace=ws, name='day1-experiment-hello')

config = ScriptRunConfig(source_directory='./src', script='run.py',
        compute_target='cpu-cluster')

run = experiment.submit(config)
```

```
aml_url = run.get_portal_url()
print(aml_url)
```

Use the URL to monitor the progress of a run.

There are additional packages that aren't installed by default, as they're required only for specific functions, for example, working with automated training or using FPGA-based deep neural networks with Azure Machine Learning Hardware Accelerated Models. You'll need a 64-bit Python environment to use automated machine learning training, as it requires the LightGBM framework. There is a thin client option, intended for use with remote automated machine learning—for example, using the tools built into Azure Machine Learning studio.

It's important to keep the SDK up to date, so you're in sync with the current set of Azure Machine Learning features. This is especially important if you're using its notebooks, which have dependencies on the service.

A good approach to using the Python SDK is to first create a model in Python using your choice of numeric methods and machine learning frameworks, with PyTorch the most common option. You'll need a model script and a training script. The training script downloads and sets up your training set and configures PyTorch for you.

Once you have these in place, create a control script that uses the SDK to build, configure, and run your model as part of an experiment in a fresh workspace. You will be able to monitor your experiment from Azure Machine Learning studio.

Azure Machine Learning and R

While Python is the popular choice for data science and machine learning, R remains popular, especially when building statistical models and analyzing big data. Microsoft offers R support across Azure as one of its main data science tools, with specialized VMs and support across its main big data platforms: Azure HDInsight and Azure Databricks, as well as inside Azure SQL Managed Instance, where you can embed R code inside your database.

R used to be a key element in the deprecated Classic Azure Machine Learning Studio, where R-based models could be used as part of your machine learning pipeline. That's changed with the launch of the newer Azure Machine Learning platform and its own drag-and-drop machine learning tools. However, R support is not completely gone, as it's supported in the currently in preview Azure CLI 2.0, which replaces the Azure Machine Learning SDK for R.

The Azure CLI's R support gives you a complete R-based training and deployment environment for your machine learning models. You will be able to call R code from the command line, working with datasets and standard R functionality.

As R is designed for statistical operations, the code needed to build and train a model can be very compact. Start by using the Azure CLI to create an appropriate compute cluster for your model. You can then define a job in YAML that loads an R container and runs your training code.

The following YAML loads an R Dockerfile and runs a generalized linear model on a set of car accident data:

```yaml
$schema: https://azuremlschemas.azureedge.net/latest/commandJob.schema.json
code:
  local_path: src
command: >
  Rscript accidents.R
  --data {inputs.training_data}
inputs:
  training_data:
    data:
      local_path: data
    mode: mount
environment:
  docker:
    build:
      dockerfile: file:Dockerfile
compute:
  target: azureml:cpu-cluster
experiment_name: r-accidents-example
description: Train a GLM using R on the accidents dataset.
```

It's very similar to working with Python, swapping it out for R and using an appropriate Dockerfile for your job. This loads the R packages needed to work with Azure.

The R code to train the model looks like this:

```r
library(optparse)

options <- list(
  make_option(c("-d", "--data_folder"), default="./data")
)

opt_parser <- OptionParser(option_list = options)
opt <- parse_args(opt_parser)

paste(opt$data_folder)

accidents <- readRDS(file.path(opt$data_folder, "accidents.Rd"))
summary(accidents)

mod <- glm(dead ~ dvcat + seatbelt + frontal + sex + ageOFocc + yearVeh
+ airbag + occRole, family=binomial, data=accidents)
summary(mod)
predictions <- factor(ifelse(predict(mod)>0.1, "dead","alive"))
accuracy <- mean(predictions == accidents$dead)
```

```
output_dir = "outputs"
if (!dir.exists(output_dir)){
  dir.create(output_dir)
}
saveRDS(mod, file = "./outputs/model.rds")
message("Model saved")
```

You can find the sample code and data for training R models in Azure Machine Learning (*https://go.microsoft.com/fwlink/?linkid=2190143*).

Build Your First Model Using Azure Machine Learning Studio

The studio is at the heart of the Azure Machine Learning platform. As well as hosting your own scripts and experiments, providing a management and training environment, it includes tooling to simplify and accelerate machine learning, using both automation and visual development environments.

Use Automated Machine Learning

Azure Machine Learning offers a useful set of low- and no-code machine learning development tools. Once you've created a machine learning workspace and assigned compute resources, you can use its automated machine learning tools to create and train a model without writing a line of code.

Start by creating a new dataset. Microsoft provides sample data in comma-separated values (CSV) format you can use to try the service out; you can either download the data to your PC (*https://aka.ms/bike-rentals*) or make a web files connection to the data from inside your studio workspace. Use the data to make a dataset, ready for consumption in Azure Machine Learning.

On the AutoML page, create a new run using your dataset. You will need to configure your training run, setting an experiment name and choosing the target column in your dataset. This will be the output data for the model and will be used to train the model, using your compute resources. Next, choose a task type from a list of basic machine learning model types: classification, regression, and time series. For most numeric models you'll want to choose regression.

You can fine-tune the task configuration, choosing the algorithms used, whether the model will be explained or not, and defining when and how a training run will end. You will want to block out most of the available algorithms, as exploring them all can take a large amount of time—and could add significant costs depending on the size of your compute cluster.

The service will run automatically once you submit your task. You can watch the models being generated in the Models tab of your workspace. Once a run has completed, depending on your exit criteria, you'll be presented with the best model and tools to help you determine if it will meet your requirements, showing the error rate, and a set of graphs that show whether predicted and actual values match.

It's worth running through a series of different trials, using different algorithms. This will allow you to find the most appropriate one for your model, comparing different runs in the studio dashboard. As each training run uses the same dataset, you have an effective baseline to compare different algorithms and sets of parameters.

Once a model is trained and ready for use, a few clicks deploy it as an inferencing service in Azure as a container or running in a Kubernetes cluster. Studio will generate appropriate endpoints for your model, with a REST API and a set of authentication keys. You can now test the resulting machine learning model in a studio notebook using Python.

Using Designer

As an alternative to writing code, you can use the no-code Azure Machine Learning designer. This gives you a drag-and-drop surface for connecting the various elements needed to process your data and then train it against various common models. The resulting pipelines bring all the necessary steps together, running them in your Azure Machine Learning workspace.

Inside studio, choose the Designer option to open the designer and create a new pipeline. The tool automatically creates and names a pipeline, ready for you to add modules, as shown in Figure 3-1. You can rename it from the default date-based name if you prefer.

Next, choose a compute resource for your model training. You can choose an existing target or create a new one. There's an option to use the same target for all your pipeline modules, or you can choose custom targets for each one. It's probably best to stick with one target, unless you have the budget to support multiple compute or GPU instances. Resources do scale down to zero when not running, but this will add time to runs when they start up.

The designer drag-and-drop canvas is similar to that used by tools like Azure Logic Apps. On the left of the screen is a set of modules that can be added to your canvas. Start by dragging on a data source, either one of your own or from a selection of sample datasets. Once these are selected, you can start to process data, using built-in data transformations to select columns for use in a model.

Connect the elements by connecting the output port of one module to the input of the next. This process builds your pipeline. Data processing modules include tools to clean up data, running cleaning algorithms and splitting out data into separate training and testing sets. You can choose the fraction of data used for each set.

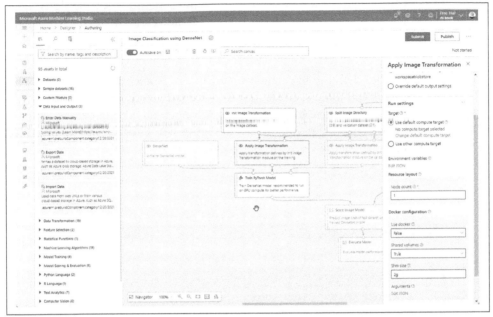

Figure 3-1. Azure Machine Learning's designer builds pipelines with drag-and-drop tooling

Next, drag on your choice of model. You get a choice of model types; choose the one that's appropriate for the type of prediction you want to make. Connect your model to a Train Model module, along with a link to your training set. This feeds into a Score module, which uses the test dataset to evaluate the resulting machine learning model.

The results of tests can be visualized, allowing you to quickly evaluate a model. If the results are good, you can quickly publish it ready for use. You have the option of producing a real-time or batch inferencing pipeline. This adds web service inputs and outputs to your pipeline and removes the training modules. You can then test the inferencing endpoints, before deploying in an Azure Kubernetes Service cluster.

Using Azure Machine Learning with Notebooks and Python

Jupyter Notebooks are an open source tool that allow you to link text, images, and code to build and share live, interactive documents. That makes them an ideal tool for data science, as you can construct series of notebooks that embed all the steps to build and run a machine learning model, alongside its documentation. There's support for many different languages, though Python is one of the most popular.

Azure Machine Learning studio can host Jupyter notebooks directly in your workspace, as well as working with both Jupyter and JupyterLab authoring environments. Notebooks get their own section of studio, with a file system for storing documents and code and a browser-hosted terminal. Finally, alongside space for your own notebooks, there's quick access to a series of notebooks that host Azure Machine Learning tutorials and samples.

To create a new file, click the file creation icon in the Notebook file browser. This lets you upload files and folders, create new folders, and create a new file. Choose to create a notebook file and give it a name. This will open an editing canvas for both code and markdown content, as you can see in Figure 3-2. The file can also be edited externally using Visual Studio Code.

Figure 3-2. Working with Python code in Azure Machine Learning Notebooks

Like all Jupyter notebooks, Azure Machine Learning's uses cells to hold code and content. You can use the integrated web-based editor to add new cells. It's based on Microsoft's Monaco editing engine (as used in Visual Studio Code), so there's full support for code completion and snippets with IntelliSense. The resulting combination is a complete Jupyter environment, with debugging tooling to manage and explore variables, making it a quick and powerful way to build and test prototypes in a collaborative space. Models can be built using any machine learning tooling with Python support—for example, calling out to both PyTorch and TensorFlow.

Python code interacts with Azure Machine Learning using the Python SDK, so you can chain a set of cells that load the SDK, log in to the service, and then set up and run an experiment, with a separate cell for your model. Microsoft provides a set of code snippets for common operations that you can use to speed up writing code, with an option to submit your choice of snippets for future use.

You can also add comments to notebooks, allowing collaboration around code. You can pick a section of code and add a comment in the comment pane. Comments give you a way to easily create and manage issues, with tools to turn them into conversation threads. Once complete, notebooks can be exported and shared using common formats, for documentation or as pure code for use in production applications.

Notebooks can be managed with tools like Git, ensuring that they can be shared and stored outside of an Azure environment. Notebooks can also be run on local Jupyter instances, allowing offline development and testing before using Azure resources to train a full-scale model. There's no need to worry about cost when editing notebooks; they connect to a compute instance only when you run a cell containing code.

Working with Azure Machine Learning Using Different Machine Learning Frameworks

Azure Machine Learning is designed to support a wide selection of different machine learning frameworks, with prebuilt compute images that simplify using them to train models. These include the popular PyTorch and TensorFlow frameworks.

PyTorch is an open source machine learning library based on the Lua-scripted Torch, developed mainly at Facebook's AI Research laboratory. It offers Python and C++ interfaces, with the Python option the most commonly used. It now also includes support for Caffe2, with support for both tensor-based and deep neural network models.

Microsoft uses PyTorch internally, with support for it in Azure Machine Learning's Python development environment. A set of prebuilt compute instances are available with the PyTorch environment, allowing you to get started quickly using tooling in the Azure Machine Learning studio. This includes using it interactively through Jupyter Notebooks or from the Azure CLI.

Azure Machine Learning also includes support for Google's open source TensorFlow. This uses Python data structures to train neural networks. As it's relatively easy to build and develop models with TensorFlow, it's become popular as a quick on-ramp to developing machine learning models. Its eager execution option works directly with NumPy linear algebra tooling, making it a logical choice for data scientists.

Like PyTorch, Azure provides prebuilt compute environments for TensorFlow, as well as support in Azure Machine Learning's Python development environments. The two frameworks work in much the same way and have similar performance characteristics. The question you need to ask when choosing which to use is what experience does your data science team have, and how close a fit is your intended workload to either option?

Start by importing the Azure Machine Learning libraries into a Python configuration script and set up a workspace using them. You'll then need to build a training script that calls either PyTorch or TensorFlow on a set of labeled data. Scripts need to be stored in your workspace along with the data.

An Azure Machine Learning PyTorch script is like any other PyTorch script. There's no need to change existing scripts to run on compute targets, so anyone who's familiar with writing PyTorch transforms and working with its parser will be able to use Azure Machine Learning. Microsoft provides sample scripts and data (*https:// go.microsoft.com/fwlink/?linkid=2190266*) to help you get started.

The same is true for TensorFlow. Again, you'll create a workspace before creating a dataset reference to your training data, which can then be registered and shared with your team. Once your dataset is registered, create a compute cluster.

The next step is to define a compute target, using the Python SDK to create a cluster. As both PyTorch and TensorFlow are focused on tensors and transforms, you should use a GPU cluster to get the best results (and to keep costs to a minimum). Microsoft provides curated environments with either PyTorch or TensorFlow preinstalled, a much easier approach than creating a VM with all the appropriate dependencies. You will be limited to Azure's currently supported version of each framework, though in practice this shouldn't make too much difference unless you plan to use new features or intend to experiment with prerelease tooling.

Alternatively, you can use the Python SDK to construct your own compute environment, using a YAML script to set up the appropriate dependencies, installing Python, and then using pip to install the tools your code needs. You will also need to define your compute environment's base image.

Once this is all in place, either via the CLI or through a set of notebooks, you can create a training job that wraps your data and your script. This will load the contents of your training folder to your compute cluster and then run a set number of training runs. You'll need to include specific details for either PyTorch or TensorFlow.

A PyTorch training script will look something like this:

```
from azureml.core import ScriptRunConfig

src = ScriptRunConfig(source_directory=project_folder,
                      script='pytorch_train.py',
                      arguments=['--num_epochs', 30, '--output_dir',
                      './outputs'],
                      compute_target=compute_target,
                      environment=pytorch_env)
```

Similarly, a TensorFlow training script will look something like this:

```
from azureml.core import ScriptRunConfig

args = ['--data-folder', dataset.as_mount(),
        '--batch-size', 64,
        '--first-layer-neurons', 256,
        '--second-layer-neurons', 128,
        '--learning-rate', 0.01]

src = ScriptRunConfig(source_directory=script_folder,
                      script='tf_train.py',
                      arguments=args,
                      compute_target=compute_target,
                      environment=tf_env)
```

You'll notice that TensorFlow requires you to define the structure of a neural network as part of its configuration, in the args section.

When run, this builds the appropriate container for your runtime and scales this across your cluster, running it on your training data. Details of the run are logged in real time to help you monitor it, with the results copied back to your workspace when done. If the model results meet expectations, you can then register it for use in Azure or download the resulting model for use locally. You also have the option of exporting it as ONNX for use with ONNX inferencing runtimes.

An Introduction to MLOps

MLOps is the application of DevOps principles to machine learning, applying the software development lifecycle to your model development, and at the same time using responsible AI techniques (see Chapter 7) to provide a governance framework for your application development. It's an important set of techniques to use if you're to make machine learning a collaborative and repeatable process, taking advantage of the built-in monitoring and tuning tools in Azure Machine Learning.

While DevOps is important for modern application development, MLOps is significantly more important for platforms like Azure Machine Learning. Models are not like code; they need maintenance to operate effectively. The more data we have, the more predictions we make; it's easier to see where our models fail and what's necessary to improve them. That data science task needs to be baked into our machine learning application development lifecycle.

Using a tool like Azure Machine Learning helps build MLOps processes into your workflow, as shown in Figure 3-3. Its pipeline approach to building and testing models gives you access to essential log file data, while tunable parameters help quickly reject failing models. It's also easy to use Azure Machine Learning to quickly package and deploy models, either as REST API endpoints, as Kubernetes-ready inferencing containers, or as cross-platform, cross-device ONNX. Integration with the Azure DevOps platform via its Azure Machine Learning allows you to start to automate the process.

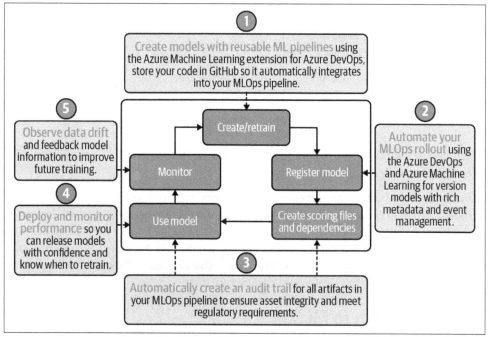

Figure 3-3. The Azure MLOps lifecycle describes how you can manage your models using the Azure Machine Learning tools

Microsoft's MLOps lifecycle has five steps:

1. Create/train/retrain your model using Azure Machine Learning studio.

2. Register the model for use in applications; use tools like GitHub and Azure DevOps to manage model versions.

3. Create scoring files and dependencies to get an audit trail for operations, to ensure regulatory compliance and give users a level of explainability for prediction results.

4. Deploy and monitor, using logs and other performance monitoring tooling to gain observability into model operations.

5. Use monitoring data to understand model drift and determine when best to retrain the model based on real-world data and metrics.

Azure provides a suite of monitoring tools that can be built into machine learning applications to improve performance, while built-in logging in Azure Machine

Learning can be used to improve models both during training and when they're running as inferencers.

Those monitoring tools can also be used to help tune models during training, to help ensure that they're initially robust and that retraining will be an infrequent process, an important requirement considering the compute and GPU requirements of training, which can be significant. The tuning tools are also an important part of the MLOps lifecycle, as they allow developers to fine-tune models and the neural networks they're built on during the training process. It's worth drilling down into these features to understand how logging can be used to tune your models.

Logging in Azure Machine Learning

Azure Machine Learning provides tools for monitoring training runs, using real-time logging via the default Python logging tools and its own custom logging tools in the SDK. You can use the MLflow logging tool to handle this data, installing the appropriate packages in your Azure Machine Learning workspace.

```
pip install mlflow
pip install azureml-mlflow
```

You can then write logging scripts that work against the Azure Machine Learning service. If you're using notebooks to build and test experiments, the resulting data can be viewed in a notebook, using Python visualization tools. Alternatively, you can get postrun visualizations via the studio, using the Experiments tab to view data and compare different runs and using filters to extract specific data. Notebooks provide tools for interactive logging, as well as widgets for displaying log data.

All the log files for a run are stored in your workspace, and you can download them for additional analysis, with a mix of text files, JSON, and log format files.

Tuning Using Hyperparameters

Logs can help provide input into tuning models through Azure Machine Learning's hyperparameters. A key element of managing the learning process, these let you tune model and neural network performance from outside your experiments. Set before learning starts, these include settings like the learning rate and the number of branches in a decision tree.

Azure Machine Learning's HyperDrive tooling can automate tuning for you, helping optimize parameters, killing poorly performing runs early, and automatically tuning neural networks to get the best configuration for your model. This includes defining the number of layers in a network and the number of nodes in each layer.

It's important to understand the deep architecture of your machine learning models before tuning their parameters. In the past this was a complex manual process that required a significant amount of compute resources. Azure Machine Learning's tooling allows you to treat tuning as an experiment, automating large parts of the process and running tests in parallel to find the best set of hyperparameters for your model.

Hyperparameter tuning experiments are written in Python using the Azure Machine Learning SDK and the HyperDrive SDK. You will need to define the search space for tuning specific hyperparameters, the metric you're using for tuning, how you will be sampling your training runs, and how your experiment can be terminated. Each run will be a complete training run in its own right, loading all the data as well as rebuilding the model.

Azure Machine Learning studio provides visualization tooling to help you determine which run was the best for your model. Its charts can be used to show correlations between your chosen metrics and hyperparameter values.

Working with hyperparameters does require a significant level of machine learning understanding, to help identify the specific parameters that will help improve your model accuracy. In practice you'll get a similar effect from using a custom model in Azure Machine Learning's automated machine learning tools.

Exporting with ONNX

Microsoft CEO Satya Nadella talks about "the intelligent cloud and the intelligent edge"; it's the combination of WinML and ONNX that powers a large portion of that edge intelligence. ONNX is an important tool for taking trained machine learning models and using them for inference on many different platforms. It allows you to develop and train models using an appropriate machine learning framework in Azure Machine Learning, and when they are ready for general use, exporting them in an ONNX format for use with a local ONNX runtime on the target system. There's support for it on everything from phones to PCs, with Windows offering its own WinML ONNX service for use in desktop applications.

You can export ONNX files from common machine learning frameworks, including PyTorch and TensorFlow. Microsoft uses ONNX internally along with the ONNX Runtime, showing significant performance gains over using alternative inferencing services.

Machine Learning doesn't only create ONNX models; if you've brought in an ONNX model from another machine learning training service or from your own systems, you can run it inside Azure Machine Learning, using it to manage and control access to your service APIs, while taking advantage of its automated inference scaling and access to Azure compute's global reach.

Using ONNX with WinML

Microsoft has built a set of inferencing APIs into the latest Windows SDKs for both Windows and Windows Server. These support working with pretrained ONNX models, allowing you to use the scale of Azure to design and train machine learning models before building them into Windows applications.

Running models locally reduces the load on networks, allowing you to put learning where it's needed, even when there's little or no bandwidth. With local ONNX models, machine learning code can run anywhere it's needed, bringing it to the edge of the network.

WinML has APIs for use with most common Windows development platforms, from native access with C and C++, to WinRT APIs for C# code. These provide abstractions from the WinML runtime and its ONNX inference engine, which works either directly with a PC's CPU or uses DirectML to take advantage of GPU processing capabilities.

When using ONNX with WinML, include the ONNX model as an asset in your project file. The techniques used to load and run the model will depend on your choice of language, but you will find using a recent build of Visual Studio provides tools for exposing model inputs and outputs, ready for use with your code. No matter what language you use, working with ONNX uses a common pattern: load, bind, and evaluate.

Your code needs to first load the model from asset storage. As ONNX models can be large, it's a good idea to build your inferencing application around an asynchronous method to handle the load. Once the model is loaded, you can bind inputs and outputs to it, making sure that your input and output classes support the expected data types. We can now iterate through our input data, calling an asynchronous evaluation method for each input value and then taking returned output data and using the results in the rest of our application.

Using WinML and ONNX, you can build standalone machine learning applications in just a few lines of code, taking trained models from Azure Machine Learning and running them anywhere you have a Windows PC or server.

Using ONNX in Machine Learning Container Runtimes

Portable machine learning systems are an important tool for edge computing, as we showed in Chapter 2, putting machine learning models where they're needed. To simplify deployment, you can package an entire ONNX runtime in a container, along with your ONNX model. Deployment is simply a matter of loading and running the container on an edge Kubernetes system like K3s or using a standalone container runtime. Updates are handled by swapping out containers with minimal service downtime and disruption.

Setting up an ONNX runtime container is easy enough. Start by building a container image that's configured with Python. Use pip to install the ONNX runtime, either for CPU or GPU. You can find Microsoft's at ONNX Runtime for Azure Machine Learning (*https://go.microsoft.com/fwlink/?linkid=2190243*). The Python ONNX runtime loads the model as an inference session, and you can use it to extract model data to enumerate inputs and outputs, as well as confirming the model metadata.

Running a model is as easy as calling your inference session with your model inputs. You can define which outputs you want to use or simply accept all responses.

Microsoft provides a prebuilt ONNX runtime container for use with pretrained Azure Machine Learning models. Based on Ubuntu 18.04 and Python 3.7, it's designed to use CPU inference and should run on most Docker or container systems. Preinstalled packages also include NumPy and Pandas, so you can work with results using common numeric methods. The prebuilt Dockerfile can be used as the foundation for your own image, adding additional libraries and code as a nested Docker image.

Wrapping It Up

In this chapter, we have explored using the tooling in Azure Machine Learning to build and train your own custom machine learning models, using common frameworks like PyTorch and TensorFlow, as well as its own no-code designer tooling. But you won't always want to build your own machine learning models, so in the next chapter we'll look at the prebuilt AI cloud services you can call as APIs: the Azure Cognitive Services.

## CHAPTER 4

Using Azure Cognitive Services to Build Intelligent Applications

In the previous chapter we looked at how a cloud service like Azure Machine Learning helps you focus on building and training machine learning models without needing to create an entire machine learning environment from scratch. But not every developer will want to build their own machine learning models, so in this chapter we're going to show you how to use ready-made AI services that you can use out of the box or customize using your own training data and call like any other API.

Using Prebuilt AI

The term "AI" is used very broadly these days and covers many different approaches, but techniques for having computers perform tasks that we used to think only people could do, like understanding and learning from experience, are fundamental. They include "cognitive" tasks like recognizing speech and images to improve customer service, detecting faces in a photo or even using a selfie to authenticate to an app, understanding speech that's full of the product names and technical terms used in your industry, or synthesizing speech from text.

Want to let your users take a photograph of a menu, translate it into another language, and get photographs showing what their food might look like? How about creating a chatbot that can deliver text and voice chat for customer support but also recognize pictures of your products that customers send in, spot whether the item is broken, and kick off the return process? Those are all powerful AI-powered features that you could build into your existing apps and tools using APIs for these cognitive tasks.

This is a fast-moving area of AI, with new algorithms and techniques being developed all the time that are complex to implement. Using prebuilt but customizable APIs that deliver cognitive tasks as a cloud service gives developers a fast way to take advantage of the business value AI can bring and give their apps a human side, without having to become data scientists. You don't have to build the model, manage the production environment for a machine learning system—or secure it.

You don't have to train the models used in Cognitive Services (although you can build custom models in some services). Microsoft delivers pretrained models as services and regularly updates them with improved training sets to ensure that they stay relevant and can work with as wide a range of source materials as possible. New and improved algorithms and models are regularly added to the different services; you may find your app gets more powerful without you needing to make any changes, or there will be new options to work with. In some cases, developers get access to new models as quickly as the teams inside Microsoft.

The Bing Search app for iOS and Android can generate speech that sounds almost exactly like a person speaking; that's important because research shows it's much less tiring to listen to results, directions, or something longer like an audiobook with the natural intonations of a human voice and with all the words articulated clearly.

Using deep neural networks to do voice synthesis and prosody (matching the patterns of stress and intonation in speech) together rather than as separate steps produces more natural and fluid speech. This is a relatively new development that was in research labs a couple of years ago, and new research papers are still coming out with refinements. But several months before the Bing team added neural voice synthesis to their mobile app, the Cognitive Services Speech API already included a preview of two neural text-to-speech voices in English, followed by Chinese, German, and Italian voices. Now companies like Progressive Insurance use custom neural voices: the Flo chatbot speaks with the voice of actor Stephanie Courtney, thanks to Cognitive Services.

Even companies with deep expertise in AI turn to these services rather than creating their own implementations. When Uber wanted to ensure the person driving the car was the registered driver who was supposed to show up as your ride, even if they'd cut their hair or changed their glasses since they got their ID photo taken, they used the Face API in Azure Cognitive Services to have drivers take a selfie on their phone. The team at Uber uses machine learning extensively and even builds open source tools for machine learning development. But they chose Cognitive Services because they were able to deliver the new feature in a few lines of code rather the months of development it would have taken to build face detection into their own platform.

The REST APIs and client SDKs (for languages including .NET, Python, Java, and Node.js) available through Azure Cognitive Services let developers use and customize the latest AI models for computer vision, text and video analytics, speech, and knowledge understanding without needing to implement, train, or host their own models. Cognitive Services can be called from Azure Functions and Azure App Service, or from within Apache Spark, Azure Databricks, Azure Synapse Analytics, and other data processing services if you need to enrich or annotate big data. (They're also available inside the Power Platform and in Logic Apps for no-code and low-code developers: we'll be covering how to use those in Chapter 6.)

As cloud services, Cognitive Services work at scale, for thousands or millions of users, reaching 150 countries, from more than 30 Azure regions around the world, with data stored and retained in compliant ways to give users control over their data. (Check out Chapter 9 for the details of what it takes to scale up machine learning services like this.) The APIs run with strict SLAs and are guaranteed to be available at least 99.9% of the time. Services are localized into multiple languages, with some services available in over 100 different languages and dialects. Speech-to-text, for example, is available in 197 and complies with ISO, SOC2, and HIPAA standards.

But you can also take some of the most useful Cognitive Services and run them locally, by building the trained model right into a smartphone app that uses the AI offload hardware on the phone, or running them in a container inside an IoT device where they can work directly with sensor readings as they're generated.

That's ideal for the remote, demanding environments where IoT devices are the most useful, and connectivity is slow, expensive, or both. This also addresses questions of data governance; if you're using image recognition to analyze medical documents for insurance, you don't have to worry about compliance issues when taking them outside the hospital network to analyze them in the cloud.

The core Cognitive Services provide skills in the areas of speech, vision, and language, including the Azure OpenAI Service, as well as services for making decisions and detecting anomalies (and you can call multiple services in the same app).

Azure Applied AI Services, which we cover in the next chapter, combine these core services into tools for common scenarios, like understanding video or processing paperwork and documents. Azure Form Recognizer uses vision and language Cognitive Services and business logic to automate dealing with forms, as you can see in Figure 4-1.

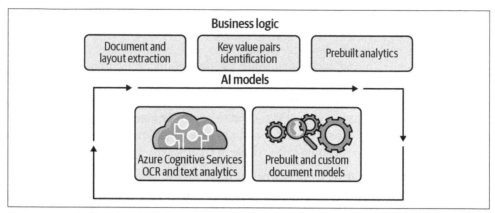

Figure 4-1. Rather than calling multiple Cognitive Services yourself to get information out of a form, you can use Azure Form Recognizer, which wraps multiple services with business logic and has pretrained models

Think of Cognitive Services as the building blocks that let any developer build an AI-powered solution: Applied AI Services add task-specific AI models and business logic for common problems like digital asset management, extracting information from documents, and analyzing and reacting to real-time data.

How to Call Cognitive Services

You don't need to sign up for an Azure account to start using Cognitive Services; you can get started with a seven-day free trial for each service. Create an Azure account and you get higher quotas and long-term commitments (with $200 in credits if you're new to Azure).

You need to create a Cognitive Services resource to start, which can be for a single service or for a combination of services: follow the quickstart instructions (*https://go.microsoft.com/fwlink/?linkid=2190268*). You will also need to authenticate all requests you make to Cognitive Services (*https://go.microsoft.com/fwlink/?linkid=2190269*).

There are SDKs for a range of popular languages and development environments to help you get started, including Python, C#, and JavaScript. With these, you can make queries using standard methods, calling APIs directly from your code. The SDKs also handle working directly with response data, formatting it in the appropriate object types. Which languages have SDKs varies from API to API, though in most cases you'll find C# SDKs available from NuGet. There's a complete list of Azure C# SDKs in this GitHub repository (*https://github.com/Azure/azure-sdk-for-net*).

The Cognitive Services features that are in the SDKs can also be accessed through REST APIs, using URLs to call the APIs with GET and POST options to handle delivering appropriate payloads to the Cognitive Service APIs.

The Azure Cognitive Services documentation (*https://go.microsoft.com/fwlink/?linkid=2190152*) has details of how to work with the various SDKs, including references for the APIs, and their header and body requirements—for example, the Computer Vision API reference (*https://go.microsoft.com/fwlink/?linkid=2190153*).

If you prefer to work with tools like Postman to build and test API queries, Microsoft provides OpenAPI Swagger definitions for Azure REST APIs. You can download those from the API references.

To illustrate the structure of a typical Cognitive Services REST API call, let's look at the uniform resource identifier (URI) for the Computer Vision service:

```
https://westcentralus.api.cognitive.microsoft.com/vision/v2.1/analyze
[?visualFeatures][&details][&language]
```

The first part of the calling URL includes the location of the API you're using, here the West Central US Azure region. Next is the Cognitive Services API group you want to call, here vision. APIs are versioned, though you should keep aware of Microsoft's deprecation and update policies to determine when to change the version your code uses. Finally, you'll see the specific API being called, along with optional configuration details. Different APIs have different versions, so don't expect them all to be versioned similarly or for different services to have the same deprecation policies. This will be used to construct a fully populated URL, like this:

```
https://{endpoint}/vision/v2.1/analyze?visualFeatures=Description,
Tags&details=Celebrities
```

Here we're calling Computer Vision's analyze function, looking for a description, and tagging the image with a list of its contents, with an additional check to see if there are any celebrities in the image.

Some APIs have a namespace that contains multiple URIs as endpoints for the different features you can call: the vision namespace in the Computer Vision API has endpoints like */detect*, */tag*, */describe* for when you want to call one specific feature. However, you will often want to call multiple features at once, and many of these functions can be grouped together when you use the */analyze* endpoint, using request parameters to choose the appropriate features you want to use.

Additional content is sent in the request body, depending on the requirements of the specific API you're using.

Not all Cognitive Services APIs have the same hierarchy; some will be calling out to Bing as well as to Azure, so ensure that you've read the documentation for the specific API you're using.

The APIs return data as JSON; you'll need to make sure that your code can parse responses and deal with any errors.

The Core Azure Cognitive Services

There are dozens of different Cognitive Services grouped into the key areas shown in Figure 4-2: speech, text, vision, and decision making, plus OpenAI. We don't have space to cover them all in detail here;[1] instead, we're going to show you how to use some of the most popular services—but you should find working with any of the APIs and SDKs a similar experience.

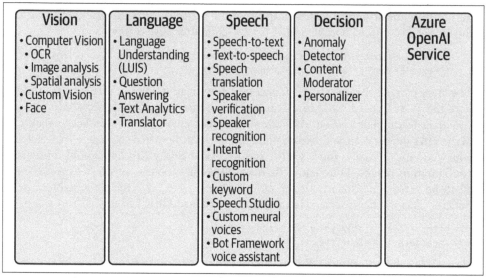

Figure 4-2. *The core Cognitive Services are grouped into five pillars*

Run Cognitive Services in Containers

Microsoft provides Docker containers for a number of Cognitive Services, although they may only have a subset of the functionality for each service, and you may need to request access (*https://aka.ms/csgate*). At the time of writing, there are containers for Anomaly Detector, Face, Form Recognizer, LUIS, Read OCR (Optical Character Recognition), Spatial Analysis, Speech language detection, Speech-to-text and Custom Speech-to-text, Text-to-speech (including custom and neural Text-to-speech), Translator, Text Analytics, Key Phrase Extraction, Text Language Detection, Sentiment Analysis, and Text Analytics for health. Check out the most up to date list (*https://oreil.ly/n3DFF*).

---

1 If you want to more details about the different Cognitive Services and how you use them, see the online documentation (*https://go.microsoft.com/fwlink/?linkid=2190271*) or check out our previous book, *Building Intelligent Apps with Cognitive APIs.*

Use containers to embed intelligence for real-time recognition and classification. If you can't send the data you want to process to the cloud because of bandwidth and latency, or because you're in a regulated environment, you can process data locally. You can export and load a trained or published Language Understanding model into a container, expose API endpoints for query prediction, and collect query logs from the container (using Fluentd) to retrain the model through the LUIS portal.

There's no transaction per second cap on Cognitive Services running in containers, so you can scale up or out as necessary to manage demand (although you have to configure Docker to allow the containers to connect with and send billing data to Azure). Using containers gives you more flexibility for versioning and updating the models you deploy. You can create a portable application architecture that you can deploy in Azure or on premises in a Kubernetes cluster, including on Azure Kubernetes Service on Azure Stack HCI.

Language

Analyze, understand, and translate text with the language APIs (or use them together with the speech services we previously mentioned).

You can turn your FAQ into an interactive chatbot with the Question Answering service, extract not just keywords but the intent of what users are saying or typing with Language Understanding, or translate in near-real time, using the terms that matter in your own business and industry. That includes full document translation, even of complex PDF files, preserving the layout and format.

Which Cognitive Services language models can you customize?

- Language Understanding (LUIS) (*https://www.luis.ai*)
- Question Answering (*https://www.qnamaker.ai*)
- Translator and Custom Translator (*https://portal.customtransla tor.azure.ai*)

The Text Analytics API takes raw text and extracts the sentiment behind the text, the key phrases it uses, the language it's written in, and the entities it refers to. A sentence refers to "Rover"; is it a dog or a car? Is "Mars" the planet or the British candy bar? Entity recognition can find time zones, temperatures, numbers and percentages, places, people, quantities, businesses, dates and times, URLs, and email addresses. There's a healthcare-specific entity recognition service that can extract medical information from unstructured documents like doctor's notes and electronic health records, detecting terms that might be a diagnosis, a condition or symptom, the name of a medicine, part of the body, and other important medical concepts.

Use sentiment analysis to filter comments and reviews from customers to feature on your site, or take the results and feed them into Power BI to generate actionable data. Use the opinion mining option to pull out subjects and opinions to get more details. If a message appears to be a complaint, you can see not only the negative sentiment rating, but also terms like "room" or "handle" and phrases like "was cold" or "broke off in my hand," allowing you to respond quickly to customer problems.

Key phrases and entities aren't enough to give you the intent of every phrase or sentence. We all have different ways of talking and typing, using different words to mean the same thing. When someone ordering a pizza through a chat interface asks for it to be delivered to their digs, what do they mean? Could they really want their pizza in a hole?

LUIS maps keywords to a list of things you expect your users to be asking for and turns a conversation into a list of ways an app or chatbot can respond.

Adding LUIS to a travel agency chatbot, for example, can narrow the information needed to help a customer. A statement like "I need a flight to Heathrow" will be parsed with the intent "BookTravel" and entities "flight" and "London." Prefilling those entities into a booking engine starts the booking process, while the chatbot prompts the user for additional information, like dates, class of travel, and the departure airport. You can see how LUIS extracts intent from a text string in Figure 4-3.

i need 2 large cheese pizzas 6 large pepperoni pizzas and 1 large supreme pizza
Q Size   Q Size   Q Size
Order
N. Sizelist   N. Sizelist   N. Sizelist

Figure 4-3. LUIS can extract both entities and intent from what someone says

LUIS is not a general-purpose machine learning model; to get the most out of it, you have to train it with domain-specific data for your industry, location, and scenarios. A set of prebuilt models for specific domains can help you get started, but they'll need additional training if you want the best results.

Translator

Microsoft Translator is a cloud-based machine translation service with multilanguage support for translation, transliteration, language detection, and dictionaries: it handles more than 100 languages and dialects. The core service is the Translator Text API, which is used in multiple Microsoft products as well as being available through Cognitive Services. The same API also powers speech translation, and we'll talk about that next.

The Translator Text API uses deep learning-powered neural machine translation, the technique that has revolutionized machine translation in the last decade, with more accurate translations that sound more natural and fluent because it translates words as part of a full sentence, rather than only looking at a few words around each target word to explain it. The translation engine also makes multiple attempts at a translation, learning from previous translation to refine the result. The result is a more human-sounding translation, particularly with non-Western languages. Check the current list of supported languages (*https://go.microsoft.com/fwlink/?linkid=2190159*).

You access the models through a REST API. While you can force operation through a specific region, Microsoft recommends using the Global option, which dynamically directs calls to any available endpoint, usually the one closest to the request location. The following Python code snippet calls a translation from English to Dutch and Brazilian Portuguese:

```python
import requests, uuid, json

subscription_key = "YOUR_SUBSCRIPTION_KEY"
endpoint = "https://api.cognitive.microsofttranslator.com"
location = "YOUR_RESOURCE_LOCATION"

path = '/translate'
constructed_url = endpoint + path

params = {
  'api-version': '3.0',
  'from': 'en',
  'to': ['nl', 'pt']
}
constructed_url = endpoint + path

headers = {
  'Ocp-Apim-Subscription-Key': subscription_key,
  'Ocp-Apim-Subscription-Region': location,
  'Content-type': 'application/json',
  'X-ClientTraceId': str(uuid.uuid4())
}

# You can pass more than one object in body.
body = [{
  'text': 'YOUR TEXT TO TRANSLATE'
}]

request = requests.post(constructed_url, params=params, headers=headers,
          json=body)
response = request.json()
```

You can have more than one target language in your translation request, with each translation in the same JSON return. The response contents indicate the detected source language and include a translation block with text and a language identifier for each selected target language:

```
[
  {
    "translations": [
      {
        "text": "TRANSLATED TEXT IN DUTCH",
        "to": "nl"
      },
      {
        "text": "TRANSLATED TEXT IN PORTUGUESE",
        "to": "pt"
      }
    ]
  }
]
```

The returned data can be parsed by your choice of JSON library.

For additional translations you can use the Dictionary Lookup API (*https://go.micro soft.com/fwlink/?linkid=2190157*), which will return alternates for the phrase you submit. The JSON data returned will have both the source and translated text, with a back translation to help you check that the translation is correct. The response will also give you details about the word or phrase you're translating.

You may also want to identify the language that's being used, so you don't waste API calls on the wrong language pairing or content that can't be translated.

Transliterating text is a useful tool for, say, converting Japanese or Chinese pictographs or Cyrillic text to a Western transliteration. In the REST request, set a from script and a to script, with the text you wish to transliterate in the JSON body. When run, the returned JSON will contain the transliterated text.

Combine the different capabilities to create your own translation service—for example, detecting Japanese text, transliterating it to Western script at the same time as translating it, while displaying any alternate translations that might be available.

The Translator Text APIs are extensible; if you need to tag only a few product names, you can apply markup to those phrases to supply the way they should be translated. But if you need translations to cover industry-specific terms, or language that's essential to your business, Custom Translator lets you extend the default translation neural network models.

 The main metric for machine translation is Bilingual Evaluation Understudy (BLEU) score: a number from 0 (the worst score) to 1 (the best); this is calculated by comparing a translation done by your model to existing reference translations done by human translators.

Custom Translator supports more than three dozen languages and lets you add words and phrases that are specific to your business, industry, or region. You can build a new translation model using "parallel" documents: pairs of documents that have already been translated so they have the same content in two languages in common formats. The service can also match sentences that are the same content in separate documents; either way, you need at least 10,000 parallel sentences. You can also supply a dictionary of specific words, phrases, and sentences that you always want translated the same way; that's useful for product names, technical terms that need to match the region, or legal boilerplate.

Training is relatively quick, on the order of a few hours, and can result in a significant improvement in both text and voice translations.

Upload dictionaries, training, tuning, and test documents for each language pair you want to use in the Custom Translator portal (*https://portal.customtranslator.azure.ai*), where you can also share access with colleagues working on the same translation project. Or you can upload training data (as shown in Figure 4-4) and leave Custom Translator to build the tuning and test sets when you click "Create model."

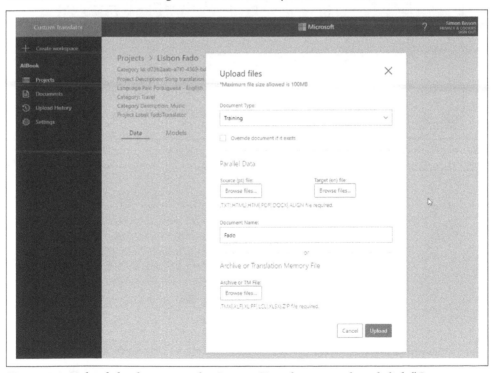

Figure 4-4. Upload the datasets to the Custom Translator portal, and click "Create model" to start training; once trained, you can see various metrics to understand the accuracy of your model

You can also add training data via an API and even use that API to build your own interfaces to the service, either adding it to your own document portal or making submission an automatic step in a document translation workflow.

As well as translating snippets of text, you can translate entire documents and keep the text formatting. Document translation works on PDF, Word, PowerPoint, CSV/Excel, Outlook messages, OpenDocument, HTML, Markdown, RTF, tab separate, and plain-text files. They can be up to 40 MB in size, in batches of up to 250 MB, but they can't be secured with a password or information protection. Store the documents in containers in Azure Blob storage (we show a suggested cloud architecture for this workflow in Figure 4-5): you can translate individual documents or the entire container.

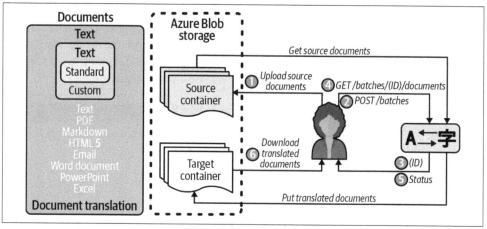

Figure 4-5. A typical Azure architecture for building a document translation workflow with Translator

 All API requests to the Document Translation service need a read-only key for authenticating access and a custom domain endpoint with your resource name, hostname, and Translator subdirectories (*https://<NAME-OF-YOUR-RESOURCE>.cognitive services.azure.com/translator/text/batch/v1.0*). This isn't the same as the global translator endpoint (api.cognitive.microsofttransla tor.com) or the endpoint listed on the Keys and Endpoint page in your Azure portal.

The translations are high quality, but you may want to use them as a first step and have a native speaker improve on them before you use them. If you do use them directly, whether it's a custom or standard translation, it's important to let your users know that the content they're reading used machine translation (and to give them a way to let you know if there are problems with the translation).

Azure OpenAI Service

If you've used the GitHub Copilot extension to generate code suggestions or had your grammar corrected while learning a language with Duolingo, you've seen OpenAI's GPT-3 large language model in action. Several Microsoft products already have features based on OpenAI. Dynamics 365 marketing uses it to suggest content to include in marketing messages. Power BI uses it to let less experienced users say in natural language what they want to do with their data and get complex DAX queries written for them (a task with a steep learning curve).

The OpenAI API lets you apply GPT-3 to a wide range of language and code tasks including extraction, classification, and translation by sending a few free text examples of what you want to see (called the prompt), which it analyses and uses for pattern matching, predicting the best text to include in the response, which is also delivered as free text. This technique is known as "in-context" learning. Context can be easily preserved by including prior responses in the text sent for each API call, so if the interface in your app allows it, users will be able to ask questions of their data iteratively.

If you want a much deeper understanding of GPT-3, check out another O'Reilly book, *GPT-3: Building Innovative NLP Products Using Large Language Models* by Sandra Kublik and Shubham Saboo.

It's useful for content generation to help a user who needs some help with creative writing or generating summaries of articles or conversations, perhaps extracting the gist of a customer support call and creating action items or triaging top issues for human review. It can search through documents to find answers to user questions, matching user query intent to how the documents are semantically related and extracting keywords or generating summaries, either to condense long text generally or to extract key points. You could create an "I don't understand this" button for education and training scenarios where OpenAI can rephrase the content in different words to help explain it. Simple ranking and answer extraction doesn't need the power of OpenAI: use it when you have more generative, open-ended questions that need the flexibility and power.

The GPT-3 models offer the best performance with English, although they have some knowledge of French, German, Russian, and other languages. Although Codex models are most capable in Python, they can generate code in over a dozen languages including JavaScript, Go, Ruby, and SQL. New iterations of the model are regularly being released, so be sure to check the documentation for the latest guidance.

You can choose from four base GPT-3 models (Ada, Babbage, Curie, and Davinci) that can understand and generate natural language, as well as the Codex series of models that can understand and generate code, turning natural language prompts into code or explaining code in natural language. Use Codex for suggesting code that developers will review and refine, or to make your internal APIs and services more accessible to less-proficient developers by explaining how they work and offering on-demand code examples:

- Ada is the fastest GPT-3 model and is a good fit for tasks that don't require too much nuance, like parsing text and correcting addresses: you could use it to extract patterns like airport codes.

- Davinci is the most capable model. It can perform all the tasks the other models can, often with fewer prompts, and delivers the best results on tasks that require more understanding of the content, like taking bullet points and generating different lengths of content like suggested headlines or marketing messages, or summarizing content in the right tone for specific audiences: you could choose a summary for schoolchildren or ask for a more business or professional tone. But it's also the largest model and requires a lot more compute power.

You can experiment with different models to see which gives you the best trade-off between speed and capability. You can also choose between different prompt approaches as you move from quick prototyping to creating a customized model that you can scale for production.

To use the service, create an Azure OpenAI resource using the same procedure as any other Azure Cognitive Service. Once the resource has been created, Azure will generate access keys and an endpoint for use from your own code.

To process text, the service first breaks the text down into chunks called tokens. One token is roughly equal to a short word or a punctuation mark.

For example, a word like "doggerel" would be tokenized as "dog," "ger," and "el," while "cat" would be a single token. The number of tokens used in a call will determine the cost and response speed of an operation. The API calls are limited by the number of tokens, which depend on the length of the input, output, and parameters. Use this OpenAI tool (*https://beta.openai.com/tokenizer*) to see how text is broken up into tokens.

Unlike other Cognitive Services, the OpenAI models use free text for input and output, using the natural language instructions and examples you provide as a prompt to set the context and predict probable next text.

This code will generate text using the Davinci natural language model, and the prompt you include will determine which of the three in-context learning techniques are used: zero-shot, few-shot, or one-shot learning.

Don't think of this as retraining the model in the usual machine learning sense—
you're providing prompts at generation time, not updating the weights in a model.
Instead, the models generate predictions about what the best text to return is, based
on the context you include in the prompt, so providing different prompts as examples
will give you different results:

```
import os
import openai

openai.api_key = os.getenv("AZURE_OPENAI_API_KEY")

response = openai.Completion.create(
  engine="text-davinci-001",
  prompt="{Customer's Prompt}",
  temperature=0,
  max_tokens=100,
  top_p=1,
  frequency_penalty=0,
  presence_penalty=0,
  stop=["\n"]
)
```

Zero-shot

You don't have to give an example in the prompt. For quick prototyping, just
state the objective and the model will generate a response. Accuracy and repeat-
ability will depend heavily on your scenario. Models fine-tuned with your own
data will let you use zero-shot prompts with greater accuracy.

Few-shot

You'll typically need a few more examples in the prompt to demonstrate the
format and the level of detail you want in the response, to make the text generated for you more relevant and reliable. There's a maximum input length, but
depending on how long examples are, you can include up to around a hundred of
them (though you may not need that many).

One-shot

Where you want to show the format for the response, but you don't expect the
service to need multiple examples, you can provide just one example.

The OpenAI Service is stochastic: even with the same prompts, you won't necessarily
get the same results every time (so if you use this in a chatbot or interface, it
should feel fresh rather than predictable). If you ask for multiple results when you
send the prompt, you can control the amount of variation in those results with the
temperature parameter: the higher the value, the more variation you'll see.

You're not guaranteed to get as many responses as you request: sometimes the response returned may be blank, so you need to check for that and handle it in your code.

Experiment with zero-, one-, and few-shot prompts from different models to see what gets you the best result, and then use the API to submit a fine-tuning job with your prompt and completion examples to get a customized model you can deploy for testing and production.

Because the OpenAI Service produces text that sounds like a human wrote it, it's important both to ensure that the content generated is appropriate for the way you're going to use it and to make sure it can't be misused. Learn how to create a responsible AI strategy for this in Chapter 7.

Speech

Speech recognition was one of the earliest areas of applied AI research, but it's only in recent years that deep learning has made it powerful enough to use widely. The very first successful implementation of deep learning instead of the traditional speech recognition algorithms was funded by Microsoft Research, helping to transform the industry. In 2017 (*https://go.microsoft.com/fwlink/?linkid=2190158*), a system built by Microsoft researchers outperformed not just individuals but a team of humans, accurately transcribing the recorded phone conversations of the industry standard Switchboard dataset.

The Azure Speech Services cover speech-to-text, text-to-speech, and real-time translation of speech in multiple languages. You can customize speech models for specific acoustic environments, like a factory floor or background road noise, and to recognize and pronounce jargon; we'll look at how to do that in the next chapter. Or you can recognize specific speakers or even use voice authentication for access and security with speaker identification and speaker verification. Speech services are available through the Speech SDK, the Speech Devices SDK, or REST APIs.

Using the Azure speech recognition tools requires working with the Cognitive Services Speech SDK. The following snippet of code loads a speech recognizer, looking for user intent in their utterances, using LUIS as a backend to the recognition process. Here we're controlling a basic home automation application, looking to turn a service on and off. The app will take the first submission from the user and use this to drive our hypothetical backend service. Finally, we check if an intent is recognized, or if valid speech is detected, before failing or cancelling operations:

```
import azure.cognitiveservices.speech as speechsdk
print("Say something...")
intent_config = speechsdk.SpeechConfig(
   subscription="YourLanguageUnderstandingSubscriptionKey",
   region="YourLanguageUnderstandingServiceRegion")
intent_recognizer =
   speechsdk.intent.IntentRecognizer(speech_config=intent_config)
model =
   speechsdk.intent.LanguageUnderstandingModel(app_id=
   "YourLanguageUnderstandingAppId")
intents = [
   (model, "HomeAutomation.TurnOn"),
   (model, "HomeAutomation.TurnOff"),
   ]
intent_recognizer.add_intents(intents)
intent_result = intent_recognizer.recognize_once()
if intent_result.reason == speechsdk.ResultReason.RecognizedIntent:
   print("Recognized: \"{}\" with intent id '{}'".format(intent_result.text,
         intent_result.intent_id))
elif intent_result.reason == speechsdk.ResultReason.RecognizedSpeech:
   print("Recognized: {}".format(intent_result.text))
elif intent_result.reason == speechsdk.ResultReason.NoMatch:
   print("No speech could be recognized:
         {}".format(intent_result.no_match_details))
elif intent_result.reason == speechsdk.ResultReason.Canceled:
   print("Intent recognition canceled:
         {}".format(intent_result.cancellation_details.reason))
```

Speech-to-text

Transcription used to require hours of time and specialized equipment for a trained human to turn speech into text, using a system that's more like drawing gestures than normal typing. It was expensive, and even commercial services don't always reach the 95% accuracy of the best human transcription.

Azure's speech-to-text tools work with real-time streamed audio data or prerecorded audio files. A single subscription covers all the Cognitive Services speech services, so you get access to translation and text-to-speech alongside the speech-to-text services.

The core speech-to-text service delivers real-time transcriptions using the same technology as Teams and Word, so it's been proven in a wide range of conditions with many accents and in multiple languages. Turn to Chapter 11 to see how it's used alongside speech translation in some very large organizations.

While you can specify the language to use, which may give more accurate recognition, the service default is a universal model with automatic language detection that works well in most situations. The list of supported languages is long and continues to grow, covering most European languages, Arabic, Thai, Chinese, and Japanese. Not all languages have the same level of available customization, but even without customizing the language model you're using, you should be able to get acceptable results in office or home applications.

Speech-to-text is available through a set of SDKs and REST APIs. As the service is primarily intended to be used with streamed data, it's easiest to use the SDKs, as these give you direct access to audio streams, including device microphones and local audio recording files. The REST APIs are useful for quick speech commands, adding speech controls to mobile apps or the web. If you've built custom language understanding models in LUIS, you can use these in conjunction with Speech Services to extract the speaker intent, making it easier to deliver what your user is asking for.

Calls to the SpeechRecognizer are run using asynchronous connections to Azure, handling connections to device microphones in the SDK and recognizing data until a set amount of silence is found. Calls can send either short speech or long utterances for recognition, and the transcribed text is delivered once the asynchronous process is complete. The SDK returns recognized speech as a string, with error handling for failed recognitions.

Text-to-speech

Speech synthesis is useful for industrial settings where users might not be able to look at a device screen—or might be wearing a HoloLens. It's also important for accessibility. Increasingly, it's also used to give products and services a recognizable voice for chatbots and other ways consumers interact with brands.

The text-to-speech services convert text into synthesized speech that's natural and sounds near human. You can pick from a set of standard and higher-quality "neural" voices, or if you want to express your brand's personality you can create your own voices.

Currently, more than 75 standard voices are available, in over 45 languages and locales. If you want to experiment with the new neural synthesized voices, you can choose between five options in four languages and locales.

Neural text-to-speech is a powerful new improvement over standard speech synthesis, offering human-sounding inflection and articulation and making computer-generated speech less tiring to listen to. It's ideal if you're using speech to deliver long-form content—for example, narrating scenes for the visually impaired or when generating audiobooks from web content. It's also a useful tool when you're expecting a lot of human interaction, for high-end chatbots or for virtual assistants. Built using deep neural networks, neural voices synthesize speech and apply patterns of stress and intonation to that speech in a single step, which makes the generated speech sound much more fluent and natural.

Standard speech synthesis supports many more languages, but it's clearly artificial. You can experiment to find the right set of parameters to give it the feel you want, tuning speed, pitch, and other settings—including adding pauses to give a more natural feel.

To get the most out of text-to-speech, you'll probably be using it in an app that calls multiple Cognitive Services: perhaps using speech recognition to extract requests from a user, passing them through LUIS to generate intents that can be used in an application, and then delivering responses using neural voices or your own custom voice. If you offer that to people as a chatbot, consider using the Azure Bot Service, which offers an integrated experience for working with those services together.

Use the Speech SDK from C# (using the .NET Standard-based SDK that works on Windows, Linux, macOS, Mono, Xamarin, UWP, and Unity), C++, Java, Go, Python, Objective-C/Swift, or JavaScript to give your applications access to speech-to-text, text-to-speech, speech translation, and intent recognition. Some versions of the SDK support different features, and you may find that more complex operations require using direct access to the Speech Service APIs.

Translation and unified speech

One of the first deep learning services that Microsoft demonstrated, when today's Cognitive Services were still just projects inside Microsoft Research, was the real-time speech translation tools. Using a modified version of Skype, an English speaker could communicate with a Chinese speaker in real time, using subtitles to translate the conversation.

Now those translation services have gone from research to product to service—for example, in the Microsoft Translator app as shown in Figure 4-6—and speech translation SDKs in Speech Services let you add real-time translation services to your C#, C++, and Java applications. Using neural machine translation techniques rather than the traditional statistical approach, this delivers much higher-quality translations using a large training set of millions of translated sentences.

The speech translation tool uses a four-step process, starting with speech recognition to convert spoken words into text. The transcribed text is then passed through a TrueText engine to normalize the speech and make it more suitable for translation. Next, the text is passed through the machine translation tools using conversation-optimized models, before being delivered as text or processed into voice through the Speech Services text-to-speech tools. The actual translation is done by the Translator Text API, which we covered in detail in "Translator" on page 56.

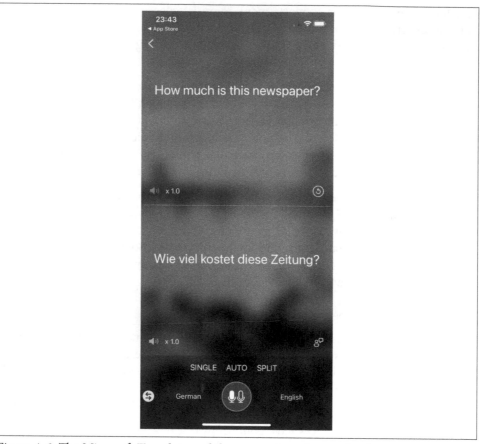

Figure 4-6. The Microsoft Translate mobile app can translate spoken language or text in a photograph

The speech translation tools work in a similar fashion to the standard speech recognition tools, using a TranslationRecognizer object to work with audio data. By default, it uses the local microphone, though you can configure it to use alternative audio sources. To make a translation, you set both source and target languages, using the standard Windows language types (even if your app doesn't run on Windows).

You'll need to install the Azure Speech Services SDK to work with the translation tools, storing your key and region details as environment variables. For Python, use:

```
pip install azure-cognitiveservices-speech
```

With that in place, set to and from languages, before running a speech recognizer and converting speech to translated text. The sample code here uses your PC's microphone to translate from French to Brazilian Portuguese. You can choose multiple target languages, especially if you're serving a diverse group of users. The translated text can be delivered to a speech synthesizer if necessary:

```
import os
import azure.cognitiveservices.speech as speechsdk
speech_key, service_region = os.environ['SPEECH__SERVICE__KEY'],
  os.environ['SPEECH__SERVICE__REGION']
from_language, to_languages = 'fr', 'pt-br'
def translate_speech_to_text():
    translation_config = speechsdk.translation.SpeechTranslationConfig(
        subscription=speech_key, region=service_region)
    translation_config.speech_recognition_language = from_language
    translation_config.add_target_language(to_language)
    recognizer = speechsdk.translation.TranslationRecognizer(
        translation_config=translation_config)
    print('Say something...')
    result = recognizer.recognize_once()
    print(get_result_text(reason=result.reason, result=result))
def get_result_text(reason, result):
    reason_format = {
      speechsdk.ResultReason.TranslatedSpeech:
        f'RECOGNIZED "{from_language}": {result.text}\n' +
        f'TRANSLATED into "{to_language}"": {result.translations[to_language]}',
      speechsdk.ResultReason.RecognizedSpeech: f'Recognized: "{result.text}"',
      speechsdk.ResultReason.NoMatch: f'No speech could be recognized:
      {result.no_match_details}',
      speechsdk.ResultReason.Canceled: f'Speech Recognition canceled:
      {result.cancellation_details}'
    }
    return reason_format.get(reason, 'Unable to recognize speech')
translate_speech_to_text()
```

Translations are delivered as events, so your code needs to subscribe to the response stream. The streamed data can either be displayed as text in real time, or you can use it to produce a synthesized translation, using neural speech if available. By working with APIs, you can produce in a few lines of code what would have been a large project if implemented from scratch. Similarly, Azure's cloud pricing model means it's economical to add speech to applications where you wouldn't have considered expensive client-side translation services.

The custom translation models we looked at as part of the language APIs are also available for translating speech.

Vision

Want to know what's in an image or a video? The different vision APIs and services can recognize faces, emotions and expressions, objects and famous landmarks, scenes and activities, or text and handwriting. You can get all the power of a fully trained image recognition deep learning network, and then you can customize it to recognize the specific objects you need with only a few dozen examples. Use that to find patterns that can help diagnose plant disease, or classify the world and narrate it to the blind, or generate metadata summaries that can automate image archiving and retrieval.

The vision APIs and technologies in Cognitive Services are the same as those that power Bing's image search and OCR text from images in OneNote and index video in Azure Streams. They provide endpoints that take image data and return labeled content you can use in your app, whether that's the text in a menu, the expression on someone's face, or a description of what's going on in a video.

As well as the APIs, there are also SDKs for many popular platforms. If you're using custom machine learning tools and analytical frameworks like Anaconda or Jupyter Notebooks, there's support for Python. Windows developers can access the Computer Vision service from .NET, JavaScript via Node.js, Android with Java, and iOS using Swift, and there's Go support for systems programming.

Behind the APIs are a set of deep neural networks trained to perform functions like image classification, scene and activity recognition, celebrity and landmark recognition, OCR, and handwriting recognition.

Many of the computer vision tasks are provided by a single API namespace, Analyze Image, which supports the most common image recognition scenarios. When you make a call to the different endpoints in the API namespace, the appropriate neural network is used to classify your image. In some cases, this may mean the image passes through more than one model, first to recognize an object and then to extract additional information. That way you can use a picture of the shelves in a supermarket to identify not only the packaging types on display but also the brands being sold and even whether the specific products are laid out in the right order on the shelf (something that's time-consuming and expensive to audit manually).

The Analyze Image API attempts to detect and tag various visual features, marking detected objects with a bounding box. Use the Vision API in the sample Cognitive Services kiosk to experiment with the API, as in Figure 4-7. Those features include:

- Tagging visual features
- Detecting objects
- Detecting brands
- Categorizing images
- Describing images
- Detecting faces
- Detecting image types
- Detecting domain-specific content
- Detecting color schemes

- Generating thumbnails
- Detecting areas of interest

You can call the Analyze Image endpoint to group many of these tasks together—for example, extracting tags, detecting objects and faces—or you can call those features individually by using their specific endpoints. Other operations, like generating thumbnails, require calling the task-specific endpoint.

Figure 4-7. Use the Vision API Explorer to see what information Analyze Image returns for an image

For more advanced requirements than simple face recognition in the Computer Vision API, use the separate Face API to compare two faces, to search by face for images of the same person in an archive, or to compare a selfie to a set of stored images to identify someone by their face instead of a password. When you want to understand movements and presence in a physical space, the Spatial Analysis APIs ingest video from CCTV or industrial cameras, detect and track people in the video as they move around, and generate events as they interact with the regions of interest you set in the space. You can use this to count the number of people entering a space, see how quickly they move through an area, or track compliance with guidelines for social distancing and mask wearing.

It's particularly important to use face recognition, spatial analysis, and video analysis services responsibly: check out the guidance in Chapter 7 for how to approach this.

To get started with Computer Vision, download the SDK, using pip. You'll also need the pillow image processing library.

```
pip install --upgrade azure-cognitiveservices-vision-computervision
pip install pillow
```

With the SDK and required components in place, you can start to write code. First import libraries, and then add your key and endpoint URL, before authenticating with the service:

```
from azure.cognitiveservices.vision.computervision import ComputerVisionClient
from azure.cognitiveservices.vision.computervision.models
    import OperationStatusCodes
from azure.cognitiveservices.vision.computervision.models
    import VisualFeatureTypes
from msrest.authentication
    import CognitiveServicesCredentials

from array import array
import os
from PIL import Image
import sys
import time
subscription_key = "PASTE_YOUR_COMPUTER_VISION_SUBSCRIPTION_KEY_HERE"
endpoint = "PASTE_YOUR_COMPUTER_VISION_ENDPOINT_HERE"
computervision_client =
    ComputerVisionClient(endpoint, CognitiveServicesCredentials(subscription_key))
```

With this in place, you're now ready to analyze an image. We'll use an image URL as a start:

```
remote_image_url = "INSERT_IMAGE_URL_HERE"
```

Our application will use the object detection feature of the Computer Vision API. Once the image has been processed, it will display details of what has been detected and where. You could use this data to quickly add overlay boxes and captions to an image:

```
print("===== Detect Objects - remote =====")
detect_objects_results_remote = computervision_client.detect_objects(remote_image_url)
print("Detecting objects in remote image:")
if len(detect_objects_results_remote.objects) == 0:
  print("No objects detected.")
else:
  for object in detect_objects_results_remote.objects:
    print("object at location {}, {}, {}, {}".format( \
```

```
object.rectangle.x, object.rectangle.x + object.rectangle.w, \
object.rectangle.y, object.rectangle.y + object.rectangle.h))
```

 Most of the computer vision tools return machine-readable information, but sometimes you need text that can be used as a caption or readout in an audio description. Call this capability either
with the */analyze* endpoint or the standalone */describe* endpoint.
Descriptions are returned as a JSON document in an ordered list in
terms of confidence, along with associated tags that can be used for
extra context.

When you request tags for an image using Image Analysis, the data returned is a
word list you can use to classify images, like making a gallery of all the images in a set
that contain car parts, or are taken outdoors. By providing multiple tags for an image,
you can create complex indexes for your image sets that can then be used to describe
the scene depicted, or find images of specific people, objects, or logos in an archive.

We can add the following snippet to our object recognition code to generate a list of
object tags along with their confidence level:

```
print("===== Tag an image - remote =====")
# Call API with remote image
tags_result_remote = computervision_client.tag_image(remote_image_url )

# Print results with confidence score
print("Tags in the remote image: ")
if (len(tags_result_remote.tags) == 0):
  print("No tags detected.")
else:
  for tag in tags_result_remote.tags:
    print("'{}' with confidence {:.2f}%".format(tag.name, tag.confidence * 100))
```

To use this API, you need to upload a still image or provide a link to an image URL.
The API returns a JSON document that contains recognized objects, along with a
confidence value you can use as a cutoff to define when to apply a tag (or when to
show the tag to your users). Pick a high threshold to avoid false positives and poor
matches cluttering up tags and search results.

Object detection also takes an image or URL; it returns the bounding box coordinates
for objects and the relationship between them: whether a "tree" is next to a "house"
or a "car" is in front of a "truck." The brand detection API is a specialized version for
product logos. If you want to improve recognition for specific classes of images, you
can train a custom vision model: we cover the steps for doing that in the next chapter.

Image categorization is a much higher-level approach than the other image classification tools: it's useful for filtering a large image set to see if a picture is even relevant
and whether you should be using more complex algorithms. Similarly, the Analyze
Image API can tell you if an image is a photo, clip art, or line art.

Decision Making

Need to detect problems and get warnings when something starts to go wrong? You can use the Anomaly Detector API for spotting fraud, telling when the sensor in an IoT device is failing, catching changing patterns in services or user activity, detecting an outage as it starts, or even looking for unusual patterns in financial markets. This is the anomaly detection Microsoft uses to monitor dozens of its own cloud services, so it can handle very large-scale data.

Designed to work with real-time or historical time series data, using individual or groups of metrics from multiple sensors, the API determines whether a data point is an anomaly and whether it needs to be delivered as an alert, without you needing to provide labeled data.

If you're using Python with the anomaly detector, you'll also need to install the Pandas data analysis library. Use pip to install it and the Azure anomaly SDK. The code snippet here also uses local environment variables to store your keys and endpoint data. Please create these before running the application. You'll also need a CSV file with time series data, giving your code a path to the data.

This code will analyze a set of time series data with a daily granularity, looking for anomalies in the data. It will then indicate where in the file an anomaly was found, allowing you to pass the data on for further analysis, alerting those responsible for the equipment or service generating the data:

```
import os
from azure.ai.anomalydetector import AnomalyDetectorClient
from azure.ai.anomalydetector.models import DetectRequest, TimeSeriesPoint,
    TimeGranularity,
    AnomalyDetectorError
from azure.core.credentials import AzureKeyCredential
import pandas as pd
SUBSCRIPTION_KEY = os.environ["ANOMALY_DETECTOR_KEY"]
ANOMALY_DETECTOR_ENDPOINT = os.environ["ANOMALY_DETECTOR_ENDPOINT"]
TIME_SERIES_DATA_PATH = os.path.join("./sample_data", "request-data.csv")
client = AnomalyDetectorClient(AzureKeyCredential(SUBSCRIPTION_KEY),
    ANOMALY_DETECTOR_ENDPOINT)
series = []
data_file = pd.read_csv(TIME_SERIES_DATA_PATH, header=None, encoding='utf-8',
    parse_dates=[0])
for index, row in data_file.iterrows():
    series.append(TimeSeriesPoint(timestamp=row[0], value=row[1]))
request = DetectRequest(series=series, granularity=TimeGranularity.daily)
print('Detecting anomalies in the entire time series.')

try:
    response = client.detect_entire_series(request)
except AnomalyDetectorError as e:
    print('Error code: {}'.format(e.error.code),
```

```
                'Error message: {}'.format(e.error.message))
     except Exception as e:
       print(e)

     if any(response.is_anomaly):
       print('An anomaly was detected at index:')
       for i, value in enumerate(response.is_anomaly):
         if value:
           print(i)
     else:
       print('No anomalies were detected in the time series.')
```

The Personalizer service uses reinforcement learning to pick what product to recommend to online shoppers, what content to prioritize for a specific visitor, or where to place an ad. It can work with text, images, URLs, emails, chatbot responses, or anything where there's a short list of actions or items to choose from, enough contextual information about the content to use for ranking, and enough traffic for the service to keep learning from. Every time a Personalizer pick is shown, the service gets a reward score between 0 and 1, based on how the shopper or reader reacted—did they click the link, scroll to the end or buy the product, pick something different or look around and then chose what was offered—that's used to improve the already-trained model. We'll see the Personalizer service in action in Chapter 12, where it powers recommendations in an online marketplace.

Content moderation

Whether you want to keep a chat room family friendly or make sure your ecommerce site doesn't offer products with unfortunate or offensive phrases printed on them, content moderation services can help. The Image and Video Indexer APIs can detect adult or "racy" content that might not be suitable for your audience. There's also an image moderation tool that can spot images that might be offensive or unpleasant, including using OCR to look for offensive language.

Images and video are uploaded to the service and passed to the Analyze Image API. Two Booleans are returned: isAdultContent and isRacyContent, along with confidence scores.

Start by installing the content moderator library via pip:

```
pip install --upgrade azure-cognitiveservices-vision-contentmoderator
```

You can now start to build a service that works with Azure to moderate content on your site. Here we're providing a list of images to check for identifiable faces:

```
import os.path
from pprint import pprint
import time
from io import BytesIO
from random import random
```

```
import uuid
from azure.cognitiveservices.vision.contentmoderator
    import ContentModeratorClient
import azure.cognitiveservices.vision.contentmoderator.models
from msrest.authentication import CognitiveServicesCredentials

CONTENT_MODERATOR_ENDPOINT = "PASTE_YOUR_CONTENT_MODERATOR_ENDPOINT_HERE"
subscription_key = "PASTE_YOUR_CONTENT_MODERATOR_SUBSCRIPTION_KEY_HERE"

client = ContentModeratorClient(
    endpoint=CONTENT_MODERATOR_ENDPOINT,
    credentials=CognitiveServicesCredentials(subscription_key)
)

IMAGE_LIST = [
    "image_url_1",
    "image_url_2"
]
for image_url in IMAGE_LIST:
    print("\nEvaluate image {}".format(image_url))
print("\nDetect faces.")
evaluation = client.image_moderation.find_faces_url_input(
    content_type="application/json",
    cache_image=True,
    data_representation="URL",
    value=image_url
)
assert isinstance(evaluation, FoundFaces)
pprint(evaluation.as_dict())
```

Content moderation isn't only for images; it can also work with text content. This can find more than adult or racy content; as well as offensive language, including looking for terms that are misspelled (maybe on purpose to evade moderation), it scans for personally identifiable information (PII) that's subject to regulation in many jurisdictions. You can add custom terms—for example, if you don't want to include posts that mention competing brands. You create the API wrapper in the same way as for images. The more comprehensive Azure Content Moderator service includes custom lists for content that's often submitted that you don't need to classify every time and can reject straight away.

 Which Cognitive Services decision models can you customize?

- Metrics Advisor (*https://oreil.ly/sR2td*) (you must be logged in to an Azure account to open this URL)

- Personalizer: customize your model in the Azure portal under Personalizer.

Wrapping It Up

In this chapter, we've looked at what you can achieve with the Azure Cognitive Services with prebuilt or customized models that you call through APIs or SDKs—but we've looked at them as separate options, and that may not be what you'll want to do in a real application. Individual Cognitive Services are powerful, but often you will want to combine multiple Cognitive Services to handle broader scenarios. You can do that yourself in code, but there are some services that developers use together so commonly that Microsoft has bundled them into Applied AI Services. Read on to learn what you can do with them.

## CHAPTER 5

Using Azure Applied AI Services for Common Scenarios

In the previous chapter we looked at the individual Cognitive Services you can use for specific tasks. Now, we're going to focus on the high-level Applied AI Services that cover common scenarios like extracting information from documents or videos.

Azure Applied AI Services

Individual Cognitive Services are powerful, but often you will want to combine multiple Cognitive Services to handle broader scenarios. If you're making a chatbot, you might start with QnA Maker but then use LUIS to make the bot better at understanding what users are trying to achieve, and use the Speech Services to let people talk to your bot as well as type. Because that's such a popular business scenario, Microsoft built the Azure Bot Service as an integrated environment that brings together all those tools.

The Bot Service is one of the Azure Applied AI Services that build on the core Cognitive Services, either combining multiple services or wrapping business logic and a UI around a single service to handle common business problems.

For example, Azure Metrics Advisor builds on the Anomaly Detector API and provides a web-based workspace that simplifies ingesting data from multiple sources and configuring settings like how sensitive you want your model to be to outliers, as well as building a graph to explain how different metrics relate to each other. As you can see in Figure 5-1, it also groups anomalies plus root cause analysis suggesting what's likely behind them with other details into an incident where you can dig into the graphs and trees of data to do your own analysis. That makes it easier to see what's going on with the metrics, when there's an anomaly, and what you should do about it;

you can also set up notifications to alert the relevant engineering, service, or business team.

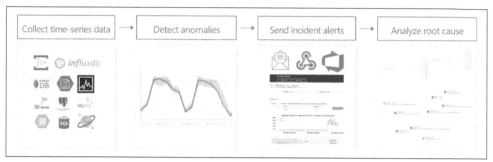

Figure 5-1. Although it uses the Anomaly Detector API, Metrics Advisor wraps the Cognitive Services API with business logic and presents it inside a web workspace

You can mark a data point as normal or anomalous to train the model as it gives you suggestions; you can also mark inflection points where a trend changes, note when time series data has seasonality (the acceptable temperature levels or delays in delivery might be very different in summer and winter), and give feedback on multiple continuous points, for cases where you can only see an anomaly in the context of the points around it.

The time series data you can analyze with Azure Metrics Advisor is ideal for tracking business metrics, IoT monitoring, or any kind of AIOps; you can spot problems as they occur and prevent outages or damage to equipment. Samsung uses Metrics Advisor to monitor the health of its Smart TV service. With multivariate analysis, you can monitor multiple systems and data sources to cover complex scenarios like smart buildings, where you might need to include temperature, room occupancy, and different heating and cooling systems to understand if unusually low levels of electricity usage mean there's a problem.

But as well as the Metrics Advisor portal where you can see all this information, you still get a REST API that you can integrate with existing analysis tools or business applications, like a dashboard of key performance indicators that you build for stakeholders.

At the time of writing, Form Recognizer is the only Applied AI Service you can run in a container on an edge device or your own servers if you have documents that you're not able to store in the cloud or you need to process documents somewhere with poor connectivity.

Azure Video Analyzer

You can extract a lot of information from videos. If you have a video library with thousands or millions of assets, using Azure Video Analyzer for Media you can extract metadata to index or control playback; use faces, emotions, and spoken words to make your videos searchable; or use the indexing to trigger automated actions. Put it all together and you can take a multi-hour video that covers a dozen topics, extract the people and topics, add captions, and put links that start the video playing in the right place next to other content that it helps to explain.

Insights are presented in a hierarchy, starting with a summary of which insights have been discovered for the video and audio (like faces, emotions, sentiments, brands, topics, or keywords) and the timecode where they occur in the video. As you drill down you can get more detailed information by querying across different insight dimensions—for example, extracting transcripts from recognized speech, lists of individuals appearing in the video, and even OCR information from text shown in the video.

The insights can cover video, audio, or both. Video insights can detect people and draw a bounding box around them in each frame to help you trace them, detect and group faces then extract thumbnail images, identify celebrities or individuals you've trained custom facial models for, identify objects and actions, and OCR text. You can use the information about people detected to do trend analysis (understanding how customers move around a store or how long they have to stand in a checkout line) or to help analyze critical events like accidents or robberies.

There are also insights specific to produced video: identifying the opening or closing credits of a show, detecting keyframes and blank frames, and marking the scenes and shots that make up a video.

Audio insights clean up noisy audio, detect language and transcribe audio (with the option of using custom language models), translate the transcript or turn it into captions, detect sounds like clapping (or silence) and emotions (based on both speech and other audio cues), or identify who speaks which words and generate statistics for how often each person speaks. Video Analyzer can also detect audio effects that aren't speech: alarms, breaking glass, barking dogs, and so on.

Combined insights extract keywords, brands, and sentiment from both speech and text shown on screen, and list the main topics covered in the video transcript.

 Find a prebuilt solution that creates a custom video search with Video Analyzer, Azure Machine Learning's Data Labeling AutoML Vision solution, Cognitive Services, and Azure Functions in this GitHub repository (*https://go.microsoft.com/fwlink/?linkid=2190161*): it's been trained to recognize breeds of dog, but you can use your own custom vision model.

In an industrial scenario where you need to enforce workplace safety, manage visual inspections, or optimize processes like turning around planes at an airport gate, Azure Video Analyzer lets you build intelligent video applications that bring together IoT solutions (using an IoT Edge module and the architecture you can see in Figure 5-2) and video analytics, without the complexity of building and operating a live video pipeline.

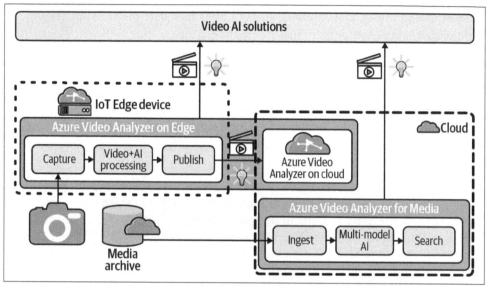

Figure 5-2. Azure Video Analyzer combines IoT at the edge with cloud AI services to help you understand what's happening in a space

When a plane lands, airport staff have to get the passengers and baggage off the plane and coordinate connecting it to local power, aircraft cleaning, safety checks, refueling, restocking the catering, and loading cargo, baggage, and passengers for the outgoing flight. Tracking that with video analytics means the airport team knows if an aircraft turnaround is taking longer than usual, so they can allocate more staff or warn the airline about potential delays, or even detect safety issues as they happen. Video Analyzer can also produce metrics to track performance over time.

You can analyze live or recorded video from existing CCTV and RTSP (Real Time Streaming Protocol) IP cameras; if you're working with live video, you can process it at the edge for high latency or record relevant video clips on the edge for limited bandwidth deployments. Video analytics use the Cognitive Services Custom Vision and Spatial Analysis APIs—plus your own custom models—to detect and track people and objects, trigger events or notifications when objects cross a line, recognize and caption speech, and mine those transcripts for insights to help you understand what's happening.

You can also see the video and analytics in Power BI by inserting the Video Analyzer player widget (*https://go.microsoft.com/fwlink/?linkid=2190275*), which makes a REST call to your Video Analyzer endpoint. You can get the embed code from the Video Analyzer portal by choosing Dashboard, Widget setup, and scrolling down to Option 2—using HTML; add your own token and insert it into a Power BI dashboard as a web content tile.

Cognitive Search

Workers still spend an average of two weeks a year looking for information, and enterprise document search is rarely as good as web search engines. You can make document search more powerful by enriching the unstructured documents you want to index and search using machine learning to extract structure, transforming information and adding metadata. That lets you classify documents by the people or organizations mentioned in them or use text to search for objects in images. New fields are added to the source documents, enriching them with, for example, entity relationships. Turn a large set of documents into a graph of information, linked by the people, products, and other entities mentioned in them, and you can go beyond just finding documents to making it easier to understand what's in them and how they're related to each other.

Azure Cognitive Search has a full-text, keyword-based search engine built on the efficient, widely used "Best Match 25" algorithm: that's great for keywords but not so good at finding the document that best matches a natural language query like "how to add a user in Exchange" or "how do I book vacation time," where lots of documents that don't answer the question will contain the keywords. So it also uses semantic search, using large transformer-based language models (the same technology used in Bing). Semantic ranking puts documents that best match the meaning of search terms rather than the exact words at the top of search results. Semantic answers extract relevant sections from the top documents, rank them for how well they answer the query, and pull the best match out of a potentially long document and highlight it at the top of the results, and semantic captions use machine reading comprehension to highlight relevant words or phrases in the previews included with search results.

Semantic search powers the search feature in Microsoft Docs, reranking the top results based on clusters of related concepts so you see a handful of very relevant results from all the documentation for that particular product or topic. In Figure 5-3, you can see how searching for a common word with multiple meanings suggests very different pages when you're reading about the visualization tools or the admin console.

Cognitive Search can handle PDFs, PowerPoints, Word documents, JPEGs, CSV and text files, and other business documents, pulling data from multiple sources including SharePoint Online indexer, Azure Files indexer, or by using Power Query connectors. It uses Cognitive Services OCR APIs to extract text from images and the Text Analytics APIs to extract key phrases, and it detects location, people, and organizations. It also includes auto-complete and spell correction, geospatial search, and faceting, which adds categories and filters to results.

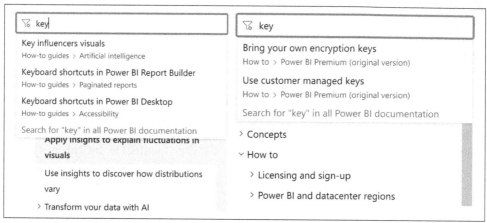

Figure 5-3. The semantic ranking feature in Cognitive Search suggests documents about using Power BI if you search for "key" when you're reading about user features but finds information about authentication keys if you're looking at admin documentation

There are SDKs for .NET, Java, Python, and JavaScript, or you can work with Cognitive Search through an API for indexing, querying, and AI enrichment. These are the key properties in a query:

queryType
> Set to "semantic" for semantic ranking and answers, "simple" or "full."

searchFields
> An ordered list of fields to apply semantic ranking on. Put the title or any summary fields first, then the URL, document body, and any other fields.

queryLanguage
> At the time of writing "en-us" is the only supported value, but this will allow multiple languages.

speller
> Set to "lexicon" for spelling correction on query terms or "none."

answers
> Set to "extractive" for semantic answers and captions or "none."

Suppose you want to highlight some information about the creator of the "imitation game" designed to test whether a computer is exhibiting intelligence behavior: Alan Turing. Here's a query for getting semantically ranked results (specifying the fields to rank) with semantic answers and captions, and any spelling mistakes in the original query automatically corrected:

```
POST https://[service name].search.windows.net/indexes/[index name]
    /docs/search?api-version=2020-06-30-preview
Your POST will need a JSON body with the query details:
{
    "search": " Where was Alan Turing born?",
    "queryType": "semantic",
    "searchFields": "title,url,body",
    "queryLanguage": "en-us",
    "speller": "lexicon",
    "answers": "extractive"
}
```

Responses are returned as JSON, ready for use in your application. Here we're showing the response for a search for Alan Turing's birthplace:

```
{
  "@search.answers": [
    {
      "key": "a1234",
      "text": "Turing was born in Maida Vale, London, while his father, Julius…",
      "highlights": " Turing was born in <strong>
      Maida Vale, London</strong> , while …",
      "score": 0.87802511
    }
  ],
  "value": [
    {
      "@search.score": 51.64714,
      "@search.rerankerScore": 1.9928148165345192,
      "@search.captions": [
        {
          "text": " Alan Mathison Turing, (born June 23, 1912,
              London, England—died June 7, 1954…",
          "highlights": " Alan Mathison Turing, (born June 23, 1912,
              <strong/>London, England</strong>—died June…",
        }
      ],
      "id": "b5678",
      "body": "…"
    },
    …
  ]
}
```

Cognitive Search isn't just about being smart with query results: you can also augment the content you're going to search. Add extra processing to further enhance documents using Cognitive Services like text translation or by calling another Applied AI Service like Form Recognizer through the Web API custom skill interface, as shown in Figure 5-4; you can also write custom skills with Azure Machine

Learning. Build a translation skill app with an HTTP trigger as an Azure Function, and whenever a new document is indexed you can automatically create a translation and have that indexed too.

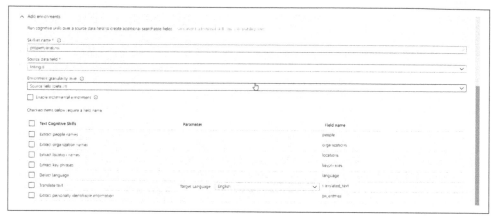

Figure 5-4. You can add cognitive skills from Azure Cognitive Services to Cognitive Search when you create your index or connect them later

 Microsoft built the JFK Files (*https://go.microsoft.com/fwlink/? linkid=2190276*) with Cognitive Search as an example of the information you can extract from large amounts of data in multiple formats. But if you were starting a project like that now, you might want to use the OpenAI Service from Chapter 4 in a skill to ask more complex questions than the JFK Files currently support.

Azure Form Recognizer

Almost every organization has to deal with forms that customers, employees, or suppliers have filled out. If you want to automate those processes, you need to be able to extract the information from paper forms that might be printed or handwritten as data that you can store in a database and use to trigger a workflow. If you have legal and financial documents like contracts and insurance quotes, they often have tables of data that you need to extract. Even though they're not forms, Azure Forms Recognizer can handle both, in over 70 languages.

In the next chapter we'll show you how business users can use this same service through the AI Builder feature in the Power Platform, where it's called form processing, but developers can also build document processing into their own application by calling the Form Recognizer REST API or client library SDKs (for C#, Java, JavaScript, and Python). You can also work with the API and SDKs to train custom models and use those in Logic Apps, Microsoft Power Automate, and Microsoft Power Apps using connectors.

Form Recognizer uses the Cognitive Services OCR, Text Analytics, and Custom Text APIs to find the fields in forms and tables and extract the text or handwriting in each field as a key-value pair, so it can spot the name field on a passport and the name shown there.

Form Recognizer has prebuilt models for invoices, sales receipts, business cards, and ID cards, or you can train custom models on your own documents to extract text and layout information. That way you can ignore the address and shipping details at the top of a shipping form, the headings on a table, and the boilerplate information at the bottom, and just pull out the fields that you need, like the invoice number, items supplied, and price.

 You can try out prebuilt, layout, and custom models in Form Recognizer with the Form Recognizer Sample Tool. You can try that out using the Form OCR Testing Tool here (*https://fott-2-1.azure websites.net*) or run it in a Docker container using this command:

```
docker pull mcr.microsoft.com/azure-cognitive-services
    /custom-form/labeltool:latest-2.1
```

The code for the tool is also available through the OCR Form Tools (*https://github.com/microsoft/OCR-Form-Tools*). To use the tool, you have to provision a Form Recognizer resource from the Azure portal and copy the API key and endpoint into the relevant fields. If you want to train a model, you'll also need Azure Blob storage for the training documents (or you can use local storage if you're running the tool in a container). Pick a file to work with and you'll see a preview of the fields, tables, and text extracted, with highlighting to show where they came from on the form. You can download the JSON output as a file. You can also deploy the Form Recognizer service in a container if you need to work with documents locally.

For documents, Form Recognizer extracts tables—including complex tables that have merged cells or no visible borders—checkboxes and similar marks like radio buttons, and both the text and structure of the document. You can see what the data looks like in Figure 5-5.

The prebuilt models extract the important information for different types of forms: the business cards model looks for name, job title, address, email, company, and phone numbers; the official ID model finds the ID number, name, country expiration, and birth dates, but on receipts it extracts all of the text, the time and date, merchant information, line items, sales tax, and totals. The invoice model also extracts all the text and looks for fields like invoice ID, customer details, vendor details, ship to, bill to, total, tax, subtotal, and line items, because it might include contractual terms or other important details. You call these models using FormRecognizerClient, which returns JSON output with RecognizedForm, FormPage, documentResults, and pageResults sections.

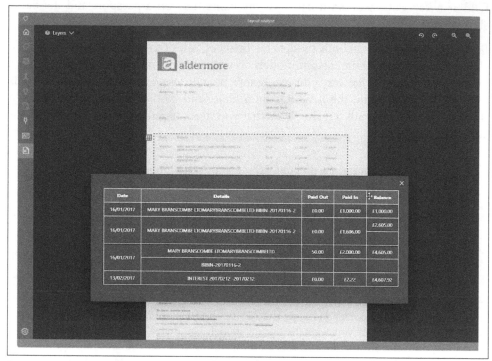

Figure 5-5. Forms Recognizer detects tables and fields in documents; this is the prebuilt model automatically extracting a table of transactions from a bank statement

Start by installing the Form Recognizer client:

```
pip install azure-ai-formrecognizer
```

Next, set variables for your endpoints and your subscription key. You're now ready to call the FormRecognizerClient with either a custom model, a pretrained receipt model, or using the default recognition settings without a specific model.

The following code snippet logs into an endpoint and attempts to recognize the content in an uploaded receipt:

```
form_recognizer_client = FormRecognizerClient(endpoint, AzureKeyCredential(key))
receiptUrl = "URL TO A RECEIPT IMAGE"

poller = form_recognizer_client.begin_recognize_receipts_from_url(receiptUrl)
result = poller.result()

for receipt in result:
  for name, field in receipt.fields.items():
    if name == "Items":
```

```
        print("Receipt Items:")
        for idx, items in enumerate(field.value):
          print("...Item #{}".format(idx + 1))
          for item_name, item in items.value.items():
            print("......{}: {} has confidence {}".format(item_name, item.value,
            item.confidence))
    else:
      print("{}: {} has confidence {}".format(name, field.value,
      field.confidence))
```

 Forms can be JPG, PNG, PDF, or TIFF files; you get the best results with text PDFs, but Form Recognizer can scan OCR text and handwriting in images and PDFs. Files must be less than 50 MB, page sizes can't be larger than A3, images must be at least 50 × 50 pixels but no larger than 10,000 × 10,000, and only the first 200 pages of long documents will be scanned.

If you have a specific form type to handle, you can train a custom model with as few as five samples (and another example to test on). You can use the graphical interface in the Form Recognizer Sample Tool or call this with the REST API using FormTrainingClient.

The following code snippet will train a recognizer model on form images stored in an Azure storage account:

```
trainingDataUrl = "PASTE_YOUR_SAS_URL_OF_YOUR_FORM_FOLDER_IN_BLOB_STORAGE_HERE"
poller = form_training_client.begin_training(trainingDataUrl,
        use_training_labels=False)
model = poller.result()
print("Model ID: {}".format(model.model_id))
print("Status: {}".format(model.status))
print("Training started on: {}".format(model.training_started_on))
print("Training completed on: {}".format(model.training_completed_on))
print("\nRecognized fields:")
for submodel in model.submodels:
  print(
    "The submodel with form type '{}' has recognized the following fields:
    {}".format(
      submodel.form_type,
      ", ".join(
        [
          field.label if field.label else name
          for name, field in submodel.fields.items()
        ]
      ),
    )
  )

# Training result information
for doc in model.training_documents:
```

```
print("Document name: {}".format(doc.name))
print("Document status: {}".format(doc.status))
print("Document page count: {}".format(doc.page_count))
print("Document errors: {}".format(doc.errors))
```

You don't necessarily need to label your forms when you train them; Form Recognizer uses unsupervised learning to understand the layout and detect the relationships between fields and entries. For many forms, that will give good enough results.

If you have more complex layouts, or fields that don't have names that Form Recognizer can use (so it has no key to assign those values to), you can train it on labeled forms; again, you need five labeled forms of the same type, with the same structure. Form Recognizer still learns the layout of the form itself, but it uses your labels for the fields and tables.

To try this out in the Form Recognizer Sample Tool, create a new custom project (you'll need the details for your Azure Blob storage container with your training data and your Form Recognizer endpoint for the connections settings). Select the Tags Editor icon in the left pane where you see the list of forms (you can see this in Figure 5-6). This extracts the text and table layout information for the documents and draws bounding boxes around the text elements. Click the table/grid icon that appears on the form to preview any table information that's been extracted.

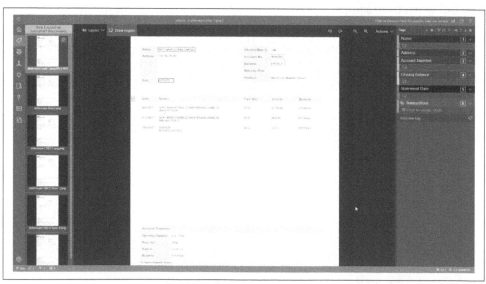

Figure 5-6. Label the fields and tables on your example forms in the Form Recognizer Sample Tool

Create tags for the key-value pairs for each field you want to extract in the tag editor pane on the right (you can set the format and data type for each tag). You can also create tags for tables (or lists of data even if they're not laid out as tables): click the icon to "Add a new table tag," then choose whether tables will have a fixed or variable number of rows and whether the labels are on the rows or columns. Mark up the individual fields in the table with format and data type.

Then select the text element or table cell you want to apply the tag to in the main editor pane in the middle and the tag to use in the tag editor pane. If the field has a label, don't include that: just the content in the field. If there are empty fields on the training form that will sometimes be filled in, label those with tags as well.

Choose the Train icon from the toolbar on the left of the window and click Train to train your custom model. When it's finished, check the average accuracy and confidence values; if they're low, you can label more documents and retrain the model. You can also click the Analyze icon in the toolbar to try out your model on a form (but don't use one of the ones you trained on).

If you have several different layouts for similar forms—invoices from different suppliers or shipping labels for different services—you can train custom models (with labels) for each of them and assign them to a composed model. That way you can call them all with a single model ID, and Form Recognizer runs a classifier to pick which model to use for the current form.

Azure Bot Service

The Azure Bot Service brings together all the different tools and services for building, testing, deploying, and managing custom chatbots—web applications with conversational interfaces—to one or more channels: that could be Facebook, Teams, embedded on your website, used in a call center, or exposed as a service through a voice assistant like Alexa or Google Assistant. See how it all fits together in Figure 5-7.

You can create bots using the Microsoft Bot Framework SDK or with the Bot Framework Composer, an IDE with a visual design surface that runs on Windows, macOS, or Linux (or in the cloud as a web application) and allows you to publish the bot directly. You can start building a bot by dragging actions onto the canvas in the Bot Framework Composer and following the prompts to integrate with Cognitive Services, or create Power Virtual Agents and then extend them through the SDK. You can even use Power Virtual Agent topics as Bot Framework skills in a bot built in Composer.

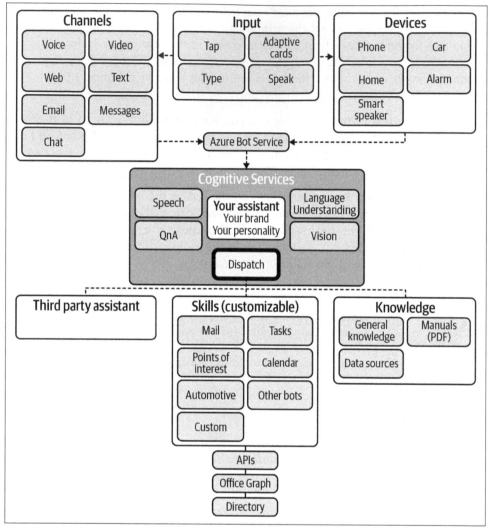

Figure 5-7. The components that make up a conversational AI experience

The Bot Service simplifies using Cognitive Services like Speech, QnA Maker, Language Understanding, and Vision in a bot so you can deal with more complicated input and understand user needs better. You can select Bot Framework skills and components from a directory using the package manager in Composer or publish your own components on NuGet and npm, or as a private feed that other bots built in your organization can incorporate.

You can track bot health and behavior with Bot Framework Analytics, which use Application Insights queries and Power BI dashboards.

If you haven't built a bot before, the Bot Framework Composer includes templates for QnA bots, bots to manage a calendar, or a full enterprise assistant bot that includes multiple capabilities. Or you can use the open source Virtual Assistant (*https://go.microsoft.com/fwlink/?linkid=2190163*) project template for C# and Type-Script, which includes business logic and handling user requests.

Immersive Reader

Dense, complex documents can be hard to follow. Some people need bigger fonts of better contrast to read on screen quickly. Use the same accessibility tool that's in Edge, Teams, and Word to make your own applications that host documents easier to read. Immersive Reader can read content aloud in a wide range of languages, translate it into even more (over 60 languages), or focus attention using highlighting and color to isolate content and make it more readable. You can see an example of how the Edge browser integrates Immersive Reader in Figure 5-8.

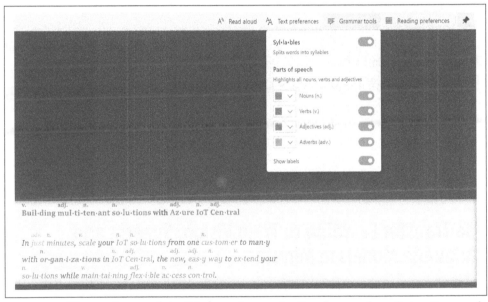

Figure 5-8. The reading mode in Edge uses Immersive Reader to reduce distractions and make it easier to focus on the text, which can also be color coded to show grammar or even translated to a different language

The Immersive Reader JavaScript library is a web application that you can integrate into a C#, JavaScript, Kotlin, Java (Android), or Swift app as an iframe; you'll also need to build a button to close the Immersive Reader UI and configure Azure AD authentication. The service parses HTML documents that are marked up with ID tags.

(While we've used Python for other examples in this book, here we're using JavaScript to go with the Immersive Reader SDK.)

You can use the SDK in web applications directly or load it via npm or Yarn for use in Node.js applications.

In a web page, use the following line to load the library:

```
<script type='text/javascript'
  src='https://contentstorage.onenote.office.net/onenoteltir
  /immersivereadersdk/immersive-reader-sdk.1.1.0.js'></script>
```

To use the library in your web page, add an HTML element to load the Immersive Reader launch button. This will invoke the SDK. You can either write Document Object Model parsing code to work with existing content on the page or load the content in chunks from other sources. Your content will need to be in a content string:

```
<div class='immersive-reader-button' onclick='launchImmersiveReader()'></div>
```

This launches the following function to display some text in Immersive Reader. You will need to pass it an authentication token and the URL of your service endpoint along with some content:

```
function launchImmersiveReader() {
  const content = {
    title: 'Immersive Reader',
    chunks: [ {
      content: 'This is Immersive Reader in action.'
    } ]
  };
  ImmersiveReader.launchAsync(YOUR_TOKEN, YOUR_SUBDOMAIN, content);
}
```

Use Transfer Learning to Train Vision, Speech, and Language Models in Minutes

Many of the Cognitive Services APIs and some of the Applied AI Services are ready to use as soon as you configure the resources; others have options for you to improve them by training with your own data. You can use prebuilt domains and dictionaries in LUIS that cover areas like music or calendar entries, and the service will learn from what your users ask. But you can also build custom dictionaries that cover the entities your users will be talking about, the things they will want to do, and the ways they're likely to phrase that intent. Similarly, you can tell Microsoft Translator about product names and terminology you use in your business to make translations more useful, or train the Form Recognizer service on the form layouts you use frequently.

For vision and speech recognition, you can train a custom model. This uses transfer learning to take a model that has already been learned by a deep neural network using a large training set and then takes off one or more of the final layers that output predictions or classifications, replacing them with new layers trained on data that covers your specific task. That way, you can take advantage of a large model that's been trained at scale and quickly adjust it to your problem with a relatively small amount of data.

Creating a Custom Vision Model

If you need to recognize images of, say, the range of products your company makes and the types of damage that occur to them, or you want to be able to find your company logo even if it's skewed because it's on the side of a truck, the standard image tagging service might not be accurate enough.

The Computer Vision API doesn't know what a leaf infected with a specific disease looks like compared to a leaf from a plant that hasn't been watered enough or a healthy egg sac in a fertilized chicken egg versus an egg that isn't developing normally. It won't be able to spot a circuit board that isn't soldered correctly or detect whether the amount of foam in treated water from an industrial process shows that it's safe for agricultural use.

The Custom Vision Service lets you build your own custom classifier based on a relatively small set of labeled images that show exactly the objects, conditions, and concepts you need to recognize. You can use it to process images that customers send you, pair it with a cheap camera to replace or supplement expensive equipment like a spectrometer, export the model to a smartphone to give employees an app that gives them point-and-click answers, or use containers to embed the trained model in a drone or smart camera for real-time recognition.

Custom Vision uses transfer learning, removing some of the final layers of a multi-layer pretrained ResNet model for specific domains (food, landmarks, retail, adult, or a general image recognition classifier) and retraining on your own set of far fewer images that you upload to the portal and tag with the objects or scenes depicted. For the best results, your training set can be as small as 30 to 50 images, ideally with a good range of camera angles, lighting, and background, variety in the size of the object, and both individual and grouped subjects. If the camera angle will be fixed, label common objects that will always be in the shot, like equipment in the background.

You can create multiple models and layer them to improve discrimination in classes that are easy to confuse (like tomatoes and bell peppers or sandwiches and layer cakes). You can build a model for detecting objects or classifying them, and sort images into single categories (multiclass classification) or apply as many tags as match the image (multilabel classification). Create the model and upload images through the Custom Vision portal (*https://www.customvision.ai*) (shown in Figure 5-9), or in code.

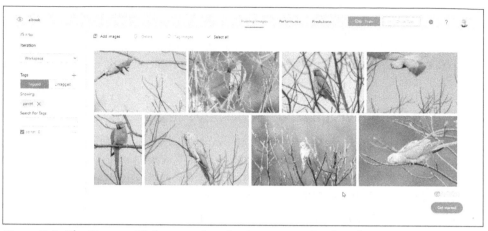

Figure 5-9. The Custom Vision portal makes it easy to upload and tag your training images

Tune when predictions are considered to be correct by setting the Probability Threshold slider. Setting the threshold high favors precision over recall (classifications will be correct, but few of them will be found); setting it low will favor recall, so most of the classifications will be found but there will be false positives. Experiment with this and use the threshold value that best suits your project as a filter when you retrieve results from the model.

 The responsible AI considerations we look at in Chapter 7 apply perhaps most strongly to image recognition, and especially to facial recognition and spatial analysis. It's important to have a balanced dataset that covers the range of objects you want to classify that doesn't introduce any false correlations (like having rulers or coins to show scale), or your custom model will perform poorly. We look at this in more detail in Chapter 8 as part of machine learning best practices, along with understanding training performance and achieving accurate, reliable results.

For challenging datasets or where you need very fine-grained classification, the Advanced Training option in the portal lets you specify how long you want the Custom Vision service to spend training the model. Once you're happy with the accuracy of a model, you can publish it as a prediction API from the Performance tab in the portal and get the Prediction URL and Prediction-Key to call in your code.

The following code snippet shows how to build a custom vision model, first tagging and uploading data, then training it. Once trained, the model can be published and used to classify images. Once you have created a resource using Custom Vision in the Azure portal, start by importing the custom vision libraries:

```
pip install azure-cognitiveservices-vision-customvision
```

This will let you add specific libraries to your code, for training and prediction. You'll need to get your various keys and endpoint details from the portal before adding them to your code.

Much of the Custom Vision service can be handled programmatically—for example, creating your training project:

```
publish_iteration_name - "classifyModel"
credentials = ApiKeyCredentials(in_headers={"Training-key": training_key})
trainer = CustomVisionTrainingClient(ENDPOINT, credentials)
# Create a new project
print ("Creating project...")
project_name = uuid.uuid4()
project = trainer.create_project(project_name)
```

You can now add your training tags to the project. Here we're going to build a model that can distinguish Airbus aircraft from Boeing's:

```
jumbo_tag = trainer.create_tag(project.id, "Boeing 747")
superjumbo_tag = trainer.create_tag(project.id, "Airbus A380")
```

You'll need a set of training images for each tag, up to 64 images per uploaded batch:

```
base_image_location = os.path.join (os.path.dirname(__file__), "Images")

print("Adding images...")

image_list = []

for image_num in range(1, 11):
  file_name = "jumbo_{}.jpg".format(image_num)
  with open(os.path.join (base_image_location, "Boeing 747", file_name), "rb")
  as image_contents:
    image_list.append(ImageFileCreateEntry(name=file_name,
    contents=image_contents.read(), tag_ids=[jumbo_tag.id]))

for image_num in range(1, 11):
  file_name = "superjumbo_{}.jpg".format(image_num)
  with open(os.path.join (base_image_location, "Airbus A380", file_name), "rb")
  as image_contents:
    image_list.append(ImageFileCreateEntry(name=file_name,
    contents=image_contents.read(), tag_ids=[superjumbo_tag.id]))

upload_result = trainer.create_images_from_files(project.id,
  ImageFileCreateBatch(images=image_list))
if not upload_result.is_batch_successful:
  print("Image batch upload failed.")
  for image in upload_result.images:
    print("Image status: ", image.status)
  exit(-1)
```

Next, we train the model. This can take some time to run:

```
print ("Training...")
iteration = trainer.train_project(project.id)
while (iteration.status != "Completed"):
  iteration = trainer.get_iteration(project.id, iteration.id)
  print ("Training status: " + iteration.status)
  print ("Waiting 10 seconds...")
  time.sleep(10)
```

Once the model is trained, it's ready to be published:

```
trainer.publish_iteration(project.id, iteration.id, publish_iteration_name,
  prediction_resource_id)
print ("Done!")
```

We can now run a prediction against the model, using images of aircraft to test its operation:

```
prediction_credentials =
  ApiKeyCredentials(in_headers={"Prediction-key": prediction_key})
predictor = CustomVisionPredictionClient(ENDPOINT, prediction_credentials)

with open(os.path.join (base_image_location, "Test/test_image.jpg"), "rb")
  as image_contents:
  results = predictor.classify_image(
    project.id, publish_iteration_name, image_contents.read())

# Display the results.
for prediction in results.predictions:
  print("\t" + prediction.tag_name +
    ": {0:.2f}%".format(prediction.probability * 100))
```

This can all be built into one application or split across separate training and prediction apps.

Running a model online has the advantage that you don't need to rebuild your app when you update a model, but local deployment may be a better choice for image and video recognition where high latency can cause problems. If you want to embed your Custom Vision classifier in an app to run it locally on a device, you can export it as TensorFlow for Android, TensorFlow.js for the web and apps built using JavaScript frameworks, CoreML for iOS 11, ONNX for WinML, or as a Windows or Linux container (that can also run on ARM hardware) with a TensorFlow model and the services necessary to call the model from Python. This means using a compact domain that may be slightly less accurate than a standard domain; if you didn't choose the compact domain to start with, you can convert to that, but you will have to retrain the model, so plan ahead if you want to use a Custom Vision model offline.

Custom Vision also supports Microsoft's Vision AI DevKit, which is a $300 smart camera development and test platform, with all the hardware you need to deploy Custom Vision models and run them on the edge of your network.

Creating a Custom Speech Model

One of the difficulties with speech recognition is the many different ways people speak. Speech styles, prosody, accents, and vocabulary vary, your field may have unusual terms, or you might need to recognize product names that could be confused for everyday words. The places speech is being recorded in can pose additional challenges; background noise at a drive-through or the acoustics of a mall or the reception desk in a building lobby are very different from someone speaking into their phone. Instead of using the default speech models, you can build a custom speech model for your specific tasks. Custom language models can be used to under-stand accents or work with specific vocabularies, building on top of the existing trained models.

 You can customize the Custom Speech, Custom Commands (for voice-controlled apps), and Custom Voice (for text-to-speech) services using the no-code Speech Studio visual environment (*https://speech.microsoft.com*) and then call them in your applications using the Speech SDK, Speech CLI, or the REST APIs.

You can then add acoustic models to account for the complexities of varied environments where accurate recognition is essential: in vehicles, on the factory floor, or out in the field. Adding a custom acoustic model will definitely be necessary if you're building code for use in a predictably noisy environment: using voice recognition in a car, or working with a specific device that might process sound in a particular way—and if you're doing that, you will likely want to run the models locally in a container. You can also build custom language models, either for a specific technical vocabulary or to improve recognition on accented speech.

For training, you can upload audio files or just text with sentences that contain jargon, technical terms, and other phrases specific to your area that might not be recognized correctly. Text training is faster—several hours rather than several days—so it's worth starting with that to see if it improves recognition enough for your needs (and not all Azure regions have dedicated hardware for audio training). To get the best results, include text that uses your specific vocabulary in different sentences and contexts that cover the ways you expect the terms to be used. You can provide up to 1.5 GB of raw text data.

For audio training, you need five or more audio files recorded in the same conditions in which your code will be recognizing speech. That means people talking in the environment or into the device you plan to use. You can also use this method to tune speech recognition to a single voice, a useful technique for transcribing podcasts or other audio sources. But if you want to recognize multiple speakers, you need recordings of a diverse collection of voices: different accents, dialects, genders, and ages, and maybe even people recorded at different times of day or when they're in a hurry, because stress affects speech patterns.

Data needs to be in 8 kHz or 16 kHz WAV files, using mono recordings. Split them up into 10- to 12-second chunks for the best results, starting and finishing with silence. Each file needs a unique name and should contain a single utterance: a query, a name, or a short sentence. Package the files in a single zipped folder that's less than 2 GB, and upload that to the Speech Services web portal shown in Figure 5-10.

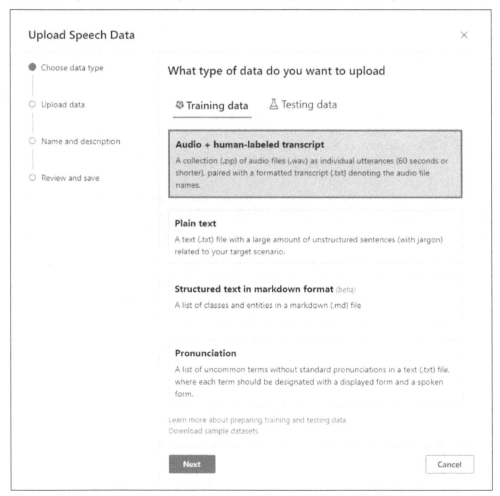

Figure 5-10. Upload speech samples and transcriptions in Speech Studio to create custom models

Each file needs to be accompanied by a transcription in the correct format: a single line of text in a file that starts with the audio filename, then a tab, then the text. Once those are uploaded, use the Speech Services portal to apply Custom Speech and pick the zipped folder as your Adaptation Data. Run the import process to add your data to the Speech Service, where it'll be processed automatically. Then you need a dataset to test it: that includes up to five hours of audio with a human-labeled transcript.

The accuracy of speech recognition is usually measured by the word error rate (WER). Count up all the mistakes the model makes—whether that's adding a word that shouldn't be there (insertions), missing a word that should (deletions), or recognizing the wrong word (substitutions)—and divide that by the number of words in the test transcript, then multiply by 100 to get the rate. If you expect to retrain your model frequently to improve accuracy, set up a CI/CD workflow to train and test models to see if the WER improves.

 Use this template (*https://go.microsoft.com/fwlink/?linkid=2190278*) to create a DevOps workflow to train, test, and release Azure Custom Speech models using GitHub Actions.

If you need to recognize what people are saying in a noisy environment or over lo-fi equipment like a walkie-talkie, you can also use your data to create a custom acoustic model: creating a new model from Azure's base models, one for directed speech and one for conversational speech, adding your own acoustic data. Custom acoustic models can work with the default speech models or with a custom recognition model.

Once your custom model is trained, deploy a custom endpoint you can call in your code.

Wrapping It Up

In this chapter, we've looked at some of the most useful prebuilt cloud AI services that are available from Azure (or, for a selection of services, running in containers on your own infrastructure) that you can call from your own apps using APIs and SDKs.

But you don't have to be a developer building applications from scratch to use Cognitive Services and Applied AI Services; several of them are also available inside Microsoft's no-code and low-code tools, the Power Platform and Logic Apps. In the next chapter, we'll look at how business users can work with developers or on their own to take advantage of these prebuilt cloud AI services for analysis, automation, and making low-code apps more powerful.

## CHAPTER 6

Machine Learning for Everyone: Low-Code and No-Code Experiences

Cloud AI services aren't only useful to professional developers who are comfortable writing code that calls APIs like the Cognitive Services we covered in Chapter 4. Business users and enterprise development teams alike are adopting low-code and no-code tools that make it easier and faster to create custom apps that use cloud AI services the same way they use storage or any other function. In this chapter we'll show you how to use AI in the Power Platform and Logic Apps. In many cases, you'll still be using Cognitive Services; you don't need to be an experienced developer to take advantage of them, but we'll also look at how those developers can bring their expertise to these platforms to help business users achieve more.

In this chapter, we show multiple ways to use AI features and services that have overlapping functionality. As always, when choosing which one you're going to use, consider what you want to achieve, what tools you're comfortable using, and where you need to get the results from any AI model you create. If you need a report with visualizations that help people understand the situation and use data to make decisions, Power BI is the place to start, but the models you use in Power BI may be built through the service or elsewhere. Power BI also has tools for preparing and transforming data that will be used in other Azure services. If you need an app or a workflow to take or automate actions that data and AI can help with, consider Power Apps and Power Automate. When you're used to working with Azure and the data you need to use machine learning with isn't stored in or accessible from the Power Platform, Logic Apps may be the right tool.

The Microsoft Power Platform

Microsoft's business application services—Power BI, Power Apps, Power Automate, and Power Virtual Agents—are known collectively as the Power Platform. Power BI is for building dashboards and reports to visualize and analyze data; Power Apps is a low-code graphical service for building responsive apps; Power Automate is for workflow and process automation (including desktop apps); and Power Virtual Agents is a guided no-code interface for creating chat bots (with low-code extensibility using the Cognitive Services–powered Bot Framework Composer).

These no-code and low-code tools are built on top of Azure services like Azure SQL, and they can be used individually or combined for analyzing data, acting on it through custom applications, automating business processes, and otherwise extending and customizing Office 365 and Dynamics 365. As you can see in Figure 6-1, they can also be extended with connectors, controls, and other components that use cloud services like Azure Functions, so more experienced developers can make them more powerful for low-code users.

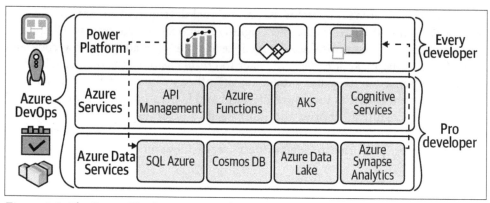

Figure 6-1. The Power Platform services depend on and integrate with many other Microsoft services that are useful for different levels of developers

The different Power Platform services take advantage of Azure AI services to process and enrich data with features like image recognition, form processing, or text classification for adding structured tags to unstructured content.

Power BI uses AI features extensively; built-in AI visuals enable natural language queries about datasets, identify outliers and key influencers in data, or help users drill in to do root cause analysis. Several Cognitive Services are integrated into Power BI for data preparation, and business analysts can create machine learning models directly in Power BI using automated machine learning for Azure Machine Learning.

Power Apps and Power Automate both include AI Builder, a wizard-like, low-code AI platform for enriching and analyzing data stored in Microsoft Dataverse that offers both prebuilt and custom AI models. Power Apps uses the same Codex model that's available in the Azure OpenAI Service to generate DAX formulas from a description of the data query you want to run. Users who are comfortable working with APIs and provisioning an Azure subscription can use Cognitive Services inside Power Apps to process the data used in an app, and Cognitive Services integration is in preview for Power Automate.

No, Low, and Pro Code

Even though it offers low-code services, the Power Platform is still relevant to professional developers. They might be working in familiar developer tools but building custom connectors to enterprise data sources, custom UI controls, or custom AI Builder or Cognitive Services models for low-code developers to use in their apps. There is also a Power Apps CLI to help them build custom components more quickly, which provides a harness for testing, debugging, and visualizing components, with built-in validations at each step.

The idea is to avoid the "cliff" common to low-code tools, when users reach the limit of the built-in options and have to ask an experienced developer to take over and reimplement the entire solution from scratch. Business and IT users can create their own apps, including AI features where they're useful, and ask a developer to help with just the extra options that they need to complete the scenario.

That means the full range of Microsoft cloud AI is available through the Power Platform for users at every skill level. The same custom models that data scientists build in Azure Machine Learning can be useful to everyone in the organization because they can use them in a Power BI report, use a custom app that relies on them to recognize photos or process forms, or call them as part of a custom workflow they create. Or you might start with the built-in AI features and move on to the more powerful AI services as you gain experience.

Power BI and AI

AI is a natural fit for business intelligence, because it's really about making better decisions based on data, and datasets are getting much bigger: web analytics, social media streams, telemetry from IoT and connected smart devices, as well as the familiar sales figures. With so much data to deal with, business intelligence tools are no longer judged on the data visualizations they provide; these are now mainstream, and it's the advanced analytics, increasingly powered by machine learning, that distinguish more powerful business intelligence approaches.

AI can help with exploring data; it can automatically find patterns in large datasets, help users understand what the data means, and predict possible future outcomes.

Gartner estimates that by 2022, 40% of machine learning model development and scoring will be done in products (like Power BI) that use machine learning rather than in tools for building machine learning systems (*Gartner Analytics and BI Magic Quadrant 2020*).

This kind of augmented analytics technology will be available widely, although it may take time for analysts to start taking advantage of it. But just as visualizations make it easier to understand the important aspects of figures, so data stories present data analysis findings in a narrative that walks people through what might be complex insights, both describing and (ideally) explaining them. As data storytelling becomes more pervasive, much of it will be created automatically by advanced analytics tools.

As you can see in Figure 6-2, Power BI has AI features for different levels of user. It already uses AI to generate insights at the data modeling layer (Quick Insights identify outliers, trends, correlation, seasonality, and other measures), uses natural language to allow users to look up data points by asking questions, and offers AI-powered visuals that you can include in reports. It can even create an entire report, including choosing and generating the visualizations for data you paste in on the Power BI web service.

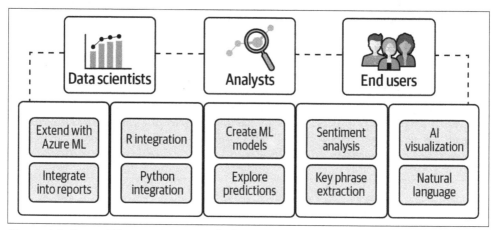

Figure 6-2. Power BI uses AI extensively for multiple features and offers appropriate tools to different levels of users

 Data brought into the Power BI online service through dataflows is stored in Azure Data Lake Storage Gen2, so data scientists and engineers can use it directly in Azure Machine Learning, Azure Databricks, and Azure SQL Datawarehouse if the low-code AI features in Power BI don't fit your needs.

You can also call Cognitive Services to enrich data or use pretrained and custom machine learning models as part of the data preparation flow.

AI Visualizations in Power BI

There are many places that you can use AI in Power BI without even realizing it, like Clustering in the Table and Scatter Chart, which discovers new measures in your data by grouping similar results. Line charts use AI to add trend lines and forecast time series. There are also specific AI-powered visualizations you can add to reports.

The Q&A visual uses natural language to let Power BI users ask questions about a report in their own words (or use the questions that the visual suggests because it's found that pattern in the data). Report authors can manage the key terms associated with the data and add synonyms to improve the language understanding for the dataset (that might be terms used inside the organization, or mapping terms like "region" and "country" if only one is used in the data). If the questions create a particularly useful visualization, you can add that to the report to reuse.

Other visuals, like the Clustered Column Chart, have Analyze or Insights buttons you can click to see an explanation of changes, like an increase or decrease in a particular figure, or to find parts of the dataset that have different distributions.

Automated Insights brings all the Power BI AI functionality together. Using code from the Cognitive Services we covered in Chapter 4 running locally in ML.NET (see Chapter 3 for how to take advantage of that for your machine learning models), it runs automatically when you open a report and shows important insights that you need to see. You can also click Get Insights in the ribbon to see any extra insights for the current visual, or add any of these AI Visualizations to a Power BI report cover:

- Key influencers helps you understand what drives an outcome, especially when you want to compare factors that you expect to affect a metric. It reasons over your data, ranks those factors, and shows you which are the key drivers.

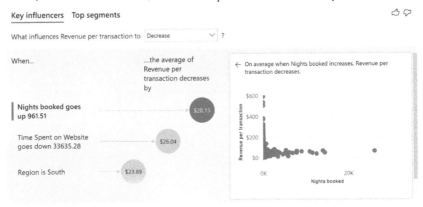

- Anomaly detection automatically detects anomalies in time series data shown in line charts. It also suggests one or more explanations for the anomalies to help you do root cause analysis.

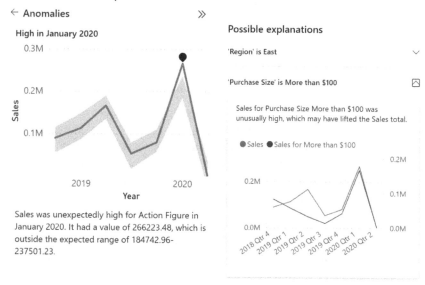

- The Decomposition Tree aggregates data and uses AI to suggest the most useful attributes to drill into across dimensions (look for the lightbulb icon as you add levels to the hierarchy). Use it to explore data to get a better idea of how it fits together, to see what you need to include in a specific visual to show a metric like what percentage of products are out of stock, or for root cause analysis.

- Smart Narratives build data stories with key takeaways and trends, explained in autogenerated text that you can edit and add extra values to.

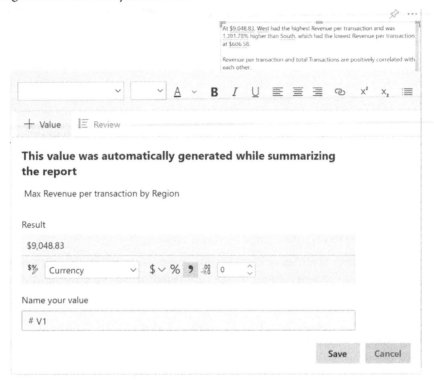

Using AI for Data Preparation in Power BI

The Power Query Editor uses AI to normalize and transform data for loading into Power BI. It can use fuzzy matching to merge similar columns, detect tables in Excel and JSON files even when the data isn't formatted as a table, or create tables from data in HTML, text, and CSV files using examples. To have Power Query work out what data transformations it needs to apply to get the same result as your examples, click Extract Table Using Examples in the Text/CSV connector dialog and fill in examples.

If you have Power BI Premium, you can call several pretrained machine learning models from Cognitive Services during data preparation. (You don't need to have a Cognitive Services subscription because the data transformation is done on the Power BI service, but you do need to enable the AI workload, which also enables AutoML).

These AI Insights are available on the Home and Add Column tabs of the ribbon in the Power Query Editor if you're using Power BI Desktop; when you're creating or editing a dataflow in the online service, use the AI Insights button in the online Power Query Editor to get the same Text Analytics and Visual models.

The first Cognitive Services integrated in Power BI are Sentiment Analysis, Key Phrase Extraction, Language Detection, and Image Tagging to extract information from documents, unstructured text, images, and sources like social media feeds. As the names suggest, they can recognize objects in images, detect language, identify key phrases, and determine positive or negative sentiment in user feedback and reviews.

AI Insights results are added as a new column in the table; if there are multiple image tags or key phrases extracted, each of them is returned on a row that duplicates the rest of the data from the original row:

- Language detection returns the language name and ISO identifier for up to 120 languages; you might want to translate the data or exclude it from further processing that's expecting a specific language.

- Key phrase extraction returns a list of key phrases found in unstructured text; it works best on larger chunks of text, while sentiment analysis, which uses machine learning classification to give a score between 0 (negative) and 1 (positive), gives better results on one or two sentences.

- Image tagging identifies objects, people, animals, actions, scenery, and locations (indoors and outdoors) in an image (uploaded or from a URL) and returns one or more tags.

Working with Custom Machine Learning Models in Power BI

You can call custom models built in Azure Machine Learning from Power BI, as long as the data scientist who creates them generates a Python schema file, publishes that with the deployed web service for the model, and grants you access to the model. They can do that in the Azure portal: you will need read access to both the Azure subscription and the Machine Learning workspace.

When you start a Power Query Editor session in Power BI Desktop or the online service, Power Query discovers all the Azure Machine Learning models you have access to and exposes them as dynamic Power Query functions. Select Azure Machine Learning from the AI Insights gallery on the Home or Add Column tabs on the ribbon to drill into those functions; you can also invoke the M functions in the Advanced Editor.

When you use a model to score data in Power BI Desktop, you'll see the predictions from the model in their own column, which you can use in reports and visualizations like any other data. The name for this is autogenerated from the model name, so you will probably want to give it a more helpful name like Predictions.

Power BI Desktop can run Python and R scripts and import the datasets they create into a data model: this can include scripts that run machine learning models.

Building Your Own Custom Models in Power BI

The data you analyze in Power BI Premium can be used for training machine learning models that can then be used to process new data in that dataflow. This uses the automated supervised machine learning capabilities in Azure Machine Learning, but you don't need an Azure Machine Learning subscription, and you build, validate, and invoke the model directly from Power BI.

AutoML is integrated into Power BI dataflows, and you can create Binary Prediction, General Classification, and Regression models. You train these with binary, category, and numeric data stored in a dataflow where the rows are labeled with the known, historical outcomes—was the invoice paid on time or not, was the risk high or low, what date was the invoice paid on. Add calculated columns for any metrics you think are strong predictors for the outcome you want to predict.

AutoML automatically splits that data into training and validation datasets, extracts the most relevant features, selects an appropriate algorithm, and tunes and validates the model. It also generates a Power BI performance report that explains how well the model is likely to perform; this shows the key influencers in the inputs that contribute to the predictions returned by the model so you can see how the predictions are made, as well as key metrics and details of the training and validation. As Figure 6-3 shows, the service walks you through the process.

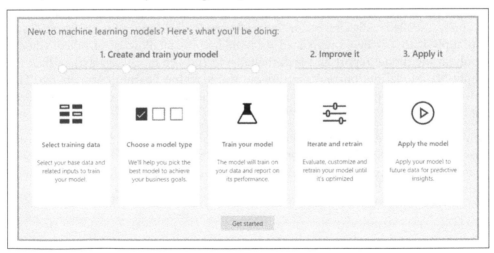

Figure 6-3. AutoML explains the steps involved in building a model before you start

Start by selecting the ML icon in the Actions column of the dataflow table, and pick "Add a machine learning model." This opens a wizard that walks you through selecting the field you want to predict and the entity it applies to (like the revenue for online visitors or the delivery date for an order). As Figure 6-4 shows, AutoML will suggest the type of model and the columns to use for an input (with warnings about any inputs that are so closely correlated with the output that they're likely to depend on it); you can change these before giving the model a name and training it.

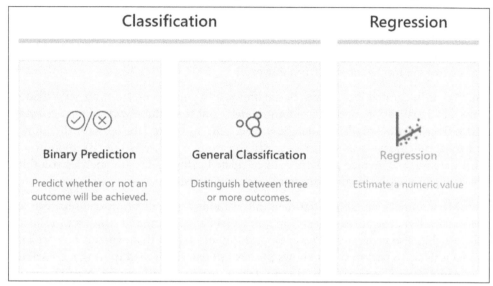

Figure 6-4. AutoML will suggest the most suitable model type (and warn you if your training data may not be suitable)

If you're satisfied with the performance shown in the report for the model, you can apply it to any new or updated data when your dataflow is refreshed. Choose Apply in the model report and pick the table to run the model against, or click the Apply ML Model button under actions in the Machine Learning Models tab. This creates two new dataflow tables: one with the predictions and one with individualized explanations for each row scored by the model.

You can also use models that other Power BI users have trained in the same workspace from the Power Query Editor in the same way you'd use models that have been shared with you from Azure Machine Learning, but you won't see explanations or training reports.

In the future, you will be able to export machine learning models from Power BI using Jupyter Notebooks (*https://github.com/micro soft/powerbi-Jupyter*), not just embed reports. That means analysts who understand an area can prototype a machine learning model, and if it proves useful and popular, they hand it over to a data scientist to work on further and standardize for more people to use.

AI Builder

Cognitive Services makes AI accessible to developers without expertise in machine learning by offering them as prepackaged APIs: AI Builder brings a subset of those same AI services to users who aren't professional developers and aren't used to calling APIs by packaging them up for low-code and no-code scenarios, so it's easy to add AI to a business process or an app.

The different services in the Power Platform are for analyzing, acting on, and automating the handling of data. AI models can be useful to all those, so the low-code AI Builder interface for training, testing, and publishing models is integrated in both Power Apps Studio and the Power Automate website.

AI Builder prediction models power some capabilities in Dynamics 365 (and the business card reader model we cover later in this chapter integrates with Dynamics because that's where the details from business cards will be particularly useful).

You can use these models to process text and images so they're more useful or to automate tasks like processing customer applications, building contact lists, filling in expense reports, taking inventory, handling basic support requests, or getting alerts for references to your products or organization on social media—but the most popular AI Builder model is forms processing.

You can also make predictions, using historical data to predict what is likely to happen in the same scenario in the future. To handle more complex scenarios, you can use multiple models together—for example, building an app for reporting incidents by submitting a photo that needs to be analyzed, tagged, and passed to the right team for response. The full set of models is shown in Figure 6-5.

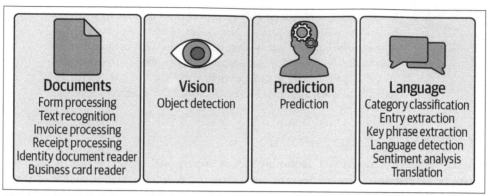

Documents	Vision	Prediction	Language
Form processing Text recognition Invoice processing Receipt processing Identity document reader Business card reader	Object detection	Prediction	Category classification Entry extraction Key phrase extraction Language detection Sentiment analysis Translation

Figure 6-5. AI Builder models fall into four main groups, and more scenarios will be included in the future

AI Builder models work on data stored in Microsoft Dataverse (the datastore for the Power Platform, previously called the Common Data Service). The service has several prebuilt models for common business scenarios that you can use without training. Some work on text: key phrase extraction, language detection (identifying what language a document is in), sentiment analysis, and translation. Others extract text from images and then process it: text recognition (OCR, including handwriting recognition), receipt processing (OCR specifically for US receipts in English), ID reader (for extracting identity information from passports and US driving licenses), and business card reader models. We'll look at how to call these models in Power Apps and Power Automate later in this chapter.

 Many, but not all, AI Builder models are built on top of Cognitive Services (the AI Builder forms processing model uses Azure Form Recognizer, for example). Just as Cognitive Services adds new features and more services regularly, in future AI Builder will get more models and extend existing models with more capabilities. At the time of writing, some models worked only with text in English and for US entities like driving licenses, but more languages and countries will be supported at a later date.

AI Builder custom models (which you train and publish yourself) are useful when you have data that's specific to your organization or scenario. They're available for prediction, form processing, and object detection, which can identify and count what's in an image. That can be common objects, products on retail shelves, or brand logos.

To make predictions, AI Builder learns the patterns in historical data and identifies when one of those patterns appears to match current data. You can use prediction models for binary outcomes like fraud detection or identifying if an account is likely to pay an invoice on time based on past payments, or for multiple outcomes like predicting whether the next shipment will be on time, early, or late. You can also predict answers that are numbers: how many items you need to keep in inventory, how many days it will take for a shipment to arrive, how many calls an agent can handle in a shift without customer satisfaction dropping. The data types for outcomes can be Yes/No, choices, a whole, decimal, or floating point number, or currency.

There are two prebuilt AI Builder models that you can customize to make them work better with your own data:

Entity extraction
Recognize specific data in text to get structured information out of a document.

Category classification
Determine what kind of information is in a document for understanding product reviews, routing requests, handling feedback, detecting spam and off-topic content, or enriching data that you want to use for predictive analysis or customer churn models.

The prebuilt entity extraction model will recognize around 25 different entities: age, weight, duration, names of people or organizations, URLs, email addresses, street addresses, cities, zip codes (in US format), US states, countries and regions, continents, phone numbers (in US format), common events, durations, days, dates and times, amounts of money, cardinal and ordinal numbers, percentages, temperatures, speeds, languages, the names of colors, and Booleans (yes or no responses). With a custom extraction model, you can modify these entity types, leave out any that aren't useful to you, or create your own.

The prebuilt classification model initially covers customer feedback and can tag text as an issue, a compliment, a customer service request, documentation, price and billing, or staff related. If you want to classify text with your own tags, you can train a custom model for up to 200 categories.

To find out if you need to train a custom model for entity extraction or classification, test the prebuilt models on your own text in Power Apps. Pick the model you're interested in and try it out by pasting in some typical data. If the results aren't accurate enough on your data, you can improve them by creating a custom model.

You can also use machine learning models from Lobe in AI Builder or bring in custom models from Azure Machine Learning (like the one we covered in Chapter 3), as shown in Figure 6-6.

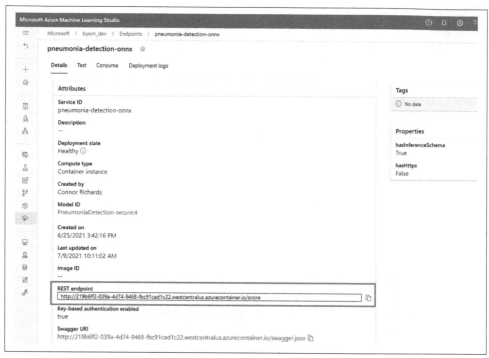

Figure 6-6. Bring your own models to AI Builder from Azure Machine Learning by calling the REST endpoint

Training a Custom Form Processing Model

The process for training the custom models in AI Builder is broadly similar: you need enough data to train the model on, and you need to store this in Dataverse.

The first step is to create the model: in Power Apps or Power Automate, open AI Builder and choose Build (if you're creating a canvas app in Power Apps, you can choose the kind of model you need and then click "New model" to open AI Builder). Pick the kind of data you want to work with (documents, text, structured data, or images) and choose what kind of information you want to extract; here we're creating a forms processing model to extract custom data from forms. Give it a name and specify where the fields, tables, and checkboxes are on the form and what they contain.

For prediction, you need to choose the outcome; for classification, you select the text and tags to use; for object detection, you specify the type of objects and the names to use for them.

Different models need different amounts of data: to train a form processing model, you need at least five sample documents in the same format (JPEG, PNG, or—preferably—PDF). If you have forms with similar information but different layouts (say, invoices from different vendors who use their own templates), you can include them in one model. You need to create names for the fields and tables you want to extract from a form; AI Builder will recognize all the fields and tables in your sample documents, and you tag each field or table cell with its name by drawing a selection around it.

> This is a technique known as "machine teaching" that shortens the machine learning training process by having a human guide the training

As you work through your examples, AI Builder may start suggesting the field or table name as it creates its model, which you can see in action in Figure 6-7; you can confirm or change these suggestions to further train it.

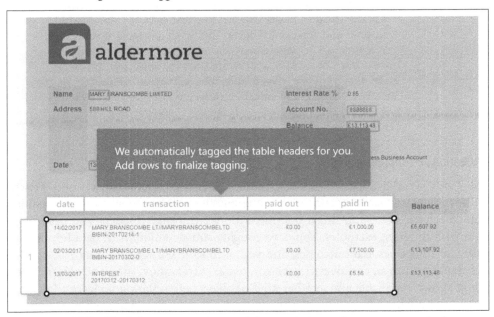

Figure 6-7. AI Builder's form processing model starts to learn from your sample documents while you're still labeling them

There are some limitations, but as a cloud service, AI Builder is getting frequent updates and improvements. Initially, forms processing was available only in English: now it handles more than 70 languages. When we started writing this chapter, forms processing didn't yet understand checkboxes on forms, it couldn't handle complex tables (where cells are merged to create a header or there's a nested table), and a table split over two pages had to be processed as two tables—but before the chapter was finished, checkboxes and complex tables were supported, and two-page tables may work by the time you read this book.

 If you're using the SharePoint Syntex service to manage large amounts of content, it integrates with AI Builder and Power Automate so you can create and use AI Builder form processing models starting from a SharePoint document library, and automate processing forms. This requires SharePoint Syntex licenses for everyone using those libraries because it allows any user with edit permissions for the library to create a forms processing model. Creating the model creates new columns in the library for the fields on the form (unless they already exist) and creates a Power Automate flow that turns the information that AI Builder extracts from the form into document metadata. Upload an image of the form to the document library and it automatically gets processed and turned into structured data in SharePoint. Forms processing is suitable for documents like invoices that have the same layout each time and for printed forms; for more complex documents like contracts that contain start and end dates, and vendor information but not in such a structured layout, you'd use the document understanding classification and extraction models in the SharePoint Syntex content center (*https://go.microsoft.com/fwlink/? linkid=2190281*) (based on the Language Understanding Cognitive Services).

Evaluating and improving models

Even with a service like AI Builder, training a custom model so it works as well as possible can take more than one attempt; the results depend on the training data you have. Once you finish training a model, you may discover you need more data with different examples. You need roughly similar amounts of data for all your different categories and outcomes, and you need to make sure the data you provide is balanced, diverse, and doesn't have accidental correlations—like one object always being shown on a table and another kind of object being photographed on the floor, unless that's where those objects will always be found. You may need photos taken in different lighting and from different angles, or text samples from different kinds of customers to get a high-quality model. We look at data quality and balancing your dataset in more detail in Chapter 8, along with other considerations for data management.

When you finish training a model for the first time, you can see the performance and quality score on the Details page; you may also be able to choose "Quick test" to see your model in action.

If you're satisfied with the quality of the model and you want to start using it, under "Last trained version," select Publish. If you think you can improve the model with more data, choose "Retrain now" to update the model. Select "New version" to create and train the model again: you can have one trained, unpublished version and one published version of each model.

How you pay for AI Builder

AI Builder is what's called a Power Platform offer: you have to have a Power Apps, Power Automate, or Dynamics 365 license that allows you to create a Dataverse environment to use AI Builder, but you also have to pay for it by how much you use it. Power Apps or Power Automate subscription licenses include some AI Builder credits, as do other Microsoft products like SharePoint Syntex, and you can buy credits in units of 1,000,000 as a monthly add-on (costing $500 at the time of writing). The credits apply to the whole Power Platform tenant, not individual users, and admins can choose whether they are available immediately or have to be assigned to the environment containing the app or flow that will use them. If a Power App that uses AI Builder to process data from, say, SharePoint, is stored in a specific environment and if you need this level of governance, you can allocate credits to that environment from the Power Platform admin center (where you can also see reports that track usage). If you're trying to estimate how much AI Builder capacity you'll need for various applications, use the AI Builder calculator (*https://go.microsoft.com/fwlink/?linkid=2190165*). For example, training and testing models and processing 1,000 forms will require something like a million credits, but it depends on the complexity of the models and how often they need retraining.

Using AI Builder Models

Most models you publish will be available in Power Apps and Power Automate for you to use yourself. If you want to make them available for other users, you need to share them from the Models page in AI Builder: this doesn't allow other people to see your training data, or to edit or retrain your model.

If someone else is going to use an app you create that uses an AI Builder model, you need to share the model as well as the app with them.

Using AI Builder in Power Automate

Power Automate is Microsoft's no-code robotic process automation tool, with a mix of standard and premium connectors. With Power Automate, you connect blocks of functionality, taking input from source connectors and routing it via optional transforms to an output.

All the AI Builder models are available to use with Power Automate as transforms. You can treat them as a template flow, using the default flows as published or modifying them to fit with your specific needs.

Once trained and tested, a model can be published ready for use in a Power Automate flow, where it appears as a connector: click "Use this in a flow" to move into the flow design screen from the AI Builder model creation tool.

For example, you can connect a flow to an email mailbox to automate a process like submitting expenses. When a message with attachments is received, use the Receipt processing model to take data from any attached receipts and feed them into an accounts system, assigned to the sender, at the same time notifying the manager responsible for expenses approvals.

AI Builder prediction models can either be scheduled to generate predictions or run immediately; in both cases, the predictions are stored in Dataverse. If you want on-demand predictions, you can create a flow in Power Automate that calls the prediction model from AI Builder in real time by choosing Predict in the Actions list that appears when you choose "New step."

Building a flow using AI Builder is similar to building any other flow. In the Power Automate menu bar, select Build to choose either a prebuilt model or train one of five different basic models: category classification, entity extraction, form processing, object detection, and prediction. You'll see that most of them are focused on working with text, as Microsoft is taking a solution-based approach to AI in the Power Platform, as shown in Power Automate's document automation tooling.

In the AI Builder screen (shown in Figure 6-8), choose a prebuilt model, like the business card reader. This pops up a wizard, with the option of using in a flow or in an app. Different models have different fields, so be careful when configuring a flow around an AI Builder model.

Pick "Use in a flow" to work with the model in Power Automate. This opens a template screen (Figure 6-9) where you can find prebuilt flows that use your chosen AI Builder connection.

Once you've deployed a prebuilt template, you can customize it to build the app you want. Starting with a template shortcuts some of the decisions needed when building a flow from scratch.

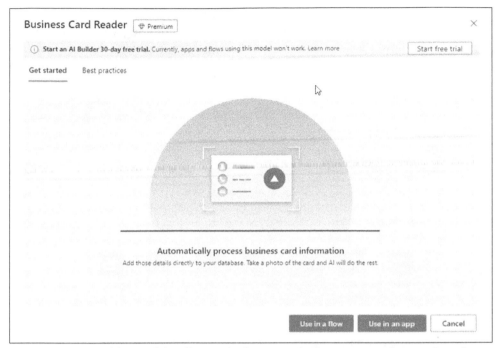

Figure 6-8. AI Builder models tell you which Power Platform services they work with

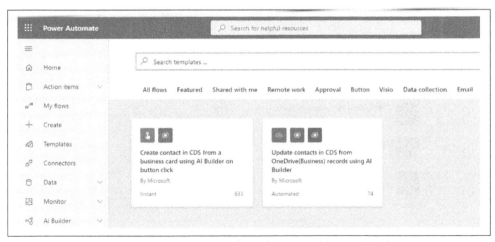

Figure 6-9. Power Automate has built-in flows for AI Builder models that you can customize

If you prefer to work with AI Builder in your own flows, it's treated like any other connector. Prebuilt models are available as connectors, offering actions that can be included in a flow. Pick the one you want from the connector selection tool (see Figure 6-10) and then continue to build your flow.

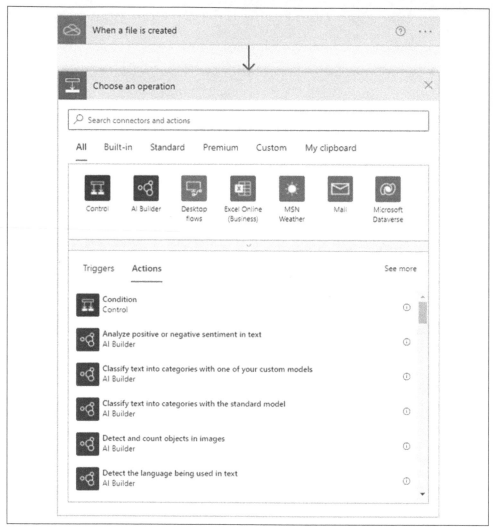

Figure 6-10. Use your AI Builder models in a flow like any other connector

There's no need to change how you work if you're using AI Builder: as far as building a flow goes, it's another connector and another set of actions you can use.

Use the Document Automation Starter Kit

AI Builder as a no-code, no-configuration way of adding machine learning to an application is part of Microsoft's aim to make it available to everyone. That means delivering solutions to common problems, and AI Builder's role in Power Automate's documentation automation service is a big part of this.

When you select the Documentation Automation starter kit in Power Automate, it launches a series of flows to process and manage custom documents. Additional modules, for invoices and receipts, are in development and may be available by the time you read this. Underneath the hood, the document automation solution is a reference implementation of a common pattern: taking documents from a mailbox, extracting data from the documents, and delivering results to a line-of-business application—for example, customer relationship management or ERP (enterprise resource planning) systems.

The resulting flow monitors mailboxes, and when mail arrives with attachments, it delivers the documents to AI Builder. Here it uses the form processing tool to extract data based on document formats you provide during setup, before passing it on to the user for validation and delivery to application APIs. As it's a Power Platform tool, it relies on Power Platform's Dataverse for document storage, using it to manage a document queue. Once run, this flow sets a state flag associated with a document to indicate that it's ready for processing.

This queue is handled by another preconfigured flow, processing document contents and extracting tagged data fields using AI Builder. This data is stored in a table in Dataverse, and once a document has been processed its state is changed to indicate that the data is being validated. You'll need to add your own validation rules in a flow and, if a document fails checks, pass it over to a Power App for manual validation. Otherwise, if the extracted data passes automatic validation, it's stored in another Dataverse table where another flow can be used to pass it on to an application.

Using AI Builder in a Power App

Power Apps offer an alternate low-code approach to working with AI Builder. You use the Power Apps tools to build an application user interface using predefined components, while connectors and actions link them to external applications and services, including AI Builder. A declarative function programming language based on Excel functions and SQL provides a way of adding business logic to your UI, linking it to data and to services and responding to user interactions.

At the time of writing, nearly all AI Builder models are available inside Power Apps (and more will be added in future):

- Business card reader
- Category classification
- Entity extraction
- Key phrase extraction
- Receipt processing
- Sentiment analysis
- Text recognition
- Form processing
- Object detection

Mostly they're available for canvas apps, which are built using standard UI components, but the business card reader model can also be used in a model-driven app, where application data models automatically create an application UI.

The invoice processing model needs a Power Automate flow, but you could invoke that flow from a Power App. AI Builder prediction models are run on demand to generate predictions that are written into your Dataverse storage, so a Power App can use those predictions like any other Dataverse data—for example, showing if a customer is likely to pay a particular invoice late alongside shipping and delivery details. If you want to have an app generate new predictions, you can create a Power Automate flow and use that in the app, but you can't call the prediction model directly from an app.

Building AI Builder into a Power App canvas app is like working with any other Power Apps component. AI Builder is available from the Insert menu, and you can grab a prebuilt model and drop it onto your application canvas. For example, the Business Card Reader drops a new control onto your canvas where you can upload an image of a card (as shown in Figure 6-11). Alternatively, you can use a custom model, training the Form processor and Object detector models for use in your application.

Once in place, add some code to the control's OnChange property to link it to a data connector. The model will extract data to a set of predefined properties that can be used to extract and transfer specific data—for example, a first name and a postal code.

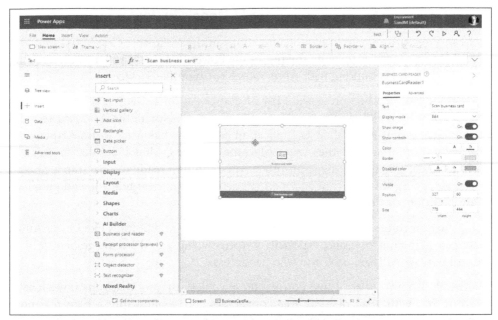

Figure 6-11. Placing the Business Card Reader AI Builder model control in a Power App

You can integrate some AI Builder models in Power Apps Studio by using the formula bar (which is where you write expressions when creating canvas apps). Currently, this is available for some language models, but it will probably include more scenarios in the future:

- Sentiment analysis
- Entity extraction
- Key phrase extraction
- Language detection
- Category classification

The formula bar has a property list showing the properties for the selected control and a formula field where you build the formula to be calculated for the selected property, which can include values, conditional formatting, application actions like navigating to a different screen in the app or running a Power Automate flow—or calling the connector to invoke an AI Builder model.

Using Cognitive Services and Other AI Models in Power Automate

You can Power Automate to handle operations in the Microsoft Graph and into and out of Azure, as well as through the rest of the Power Platform and its Dataverse data layer. That includes working with AI services like Cognitive Services.

If a service has an API, you can use it with Power Automate, either using a prebuilt connector or by building your own custom connectors. Not all the AI-based services are obvious; some are bundled as application endpoints, like Microsoft's AI-powered Translator. If you've used the Azure Machine Learning Model Builder to create a custom model, you'll have the appropriate API definition ready to turn into a custom connector, going straight from an OpenAPI definition to a module you can plug into a Power Automate flow.

Using custom connectors with low- and no-code development tools like Power Automate can help control usage, especially if you're using an API management tool to control how AI APIs are used and who has access.

Microsoft also now offers a free Power Automate desktop tool that runs flows locally on your PC, with a set of basic free connectors and a subscription plan for more complex operations. This offers a subset of the Azure Cognitive Services APIs, with basic computer vision and text analytics tooling. It can also be used as a trigger for cloud-hosted Power Automate flows, providing local processing before passing data on to the service.

Power Automate offers a set of Cognitive Services connectors, some of which are still in preview. These provide simplified access to the APIs, supporting most common uses. You will need a Cognitive Services account key to use them, and there are limits that prevent you from using them for complex tasks. For example, the Computer Vision connector can only be used 1,200 times per connection, with limits renewing every 60 seconds. That means you wouldn't use it on a video feed, but you could use it as part of a Power Automate flow that was being used to see if supermarket shelves need stacking. More complex connectors have lower limits, so be careful to read the documentation before you deploy an application. If you need to go outside the limits, it may well be worth considering using the Cognitive Services APIs directly, in a traditional application.

The various Cognitive Services connectors offer most of the same services as the Azure APIs. Once you drop a connector into a flow, you can configure the supported services, choosing the appropriate operation and configuring the connector parameters. You should treat each connector as a single function application; so, if you're using the Face ID connector, you'll need separate flows to add new faces and to detect a person from an image.

Microsoft simplifies getting started with its Cognitive Services connectors by providing a set of templates. These have been developed by Microsoft or the Power

Automate community and cover a set of common scenarios. For example, one offers simple OCR, converting an image into a text-based PDF and storing it in OneDrive. You can use these templates as quick starts, experimenting with the services they offer and then using them as the basis of your own applications. Templates like these provide an effective hands-on learning environment, showing how AI-powered flows can be built and used.

Currently, Microsoft provides preconfigured connectors for the following Cognitive Services:

- Computer Vision
- Content Moderator (in preview)
- Custom Vision (in preview)
- Face API (in preview)
- LUIS (in preview)
- Translator V2 (in preview)
- QnA Maker (in preview)
- Form Recognizer (in preview)
- Text Analytics (in preview)
- Video Indexer (in preview)

While most of the services are available as previews, they are ready to use and there should be no changes to their parameters and operations.

All the Cognitive Services connectors are designed to be used in the middle of a flow; they don't provide triggers, and they do deliver outputs that can be used by other connectors.

You can put together an AI-powered Power Automate flow in a handful of steps. In the following example, we're creating one that will monitor a OneDrive for Business folder for uploaded image files and then identify objects in the image, using the Computer Vision connector.

First, log into Power Automate and create a flow. Start by giving it a name, and choose an initial trigger (see Figure 6-12). You can search for a trigger or select from a list of commonly used triggers. We'll choose to trigger our flow on file creation in OneDrive for Business.

Once you've created a flow, you'll be taken to the Power Automate graphical editor. This will show you your trigger, ready for you to log into OneDrive and choose a folder to monitor. You will need to create the folder in OneDrive and then pick it from a drop-down menu in Power Automate (shown in Figure 6-13).

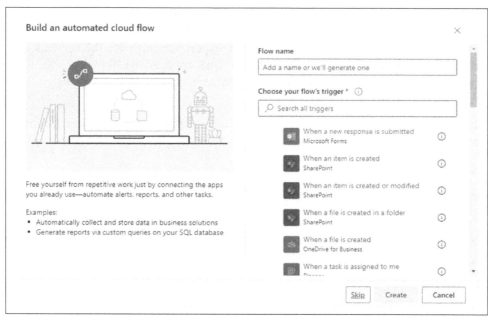

Figure 6-12. To start a new Power Automate flow, choose your trigger

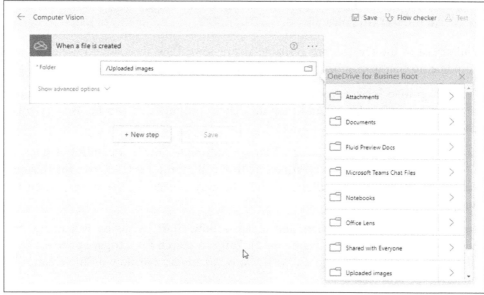

Figure 6-13. Choose the OneDrive folder where the images to be recognized are stored

Next, add a Computer Vision connector by searching for it in the "New step" dialog. You'll need to create a resource in an Azure account for this, as shown in Figure 6-14, but it's available in the Free tier.

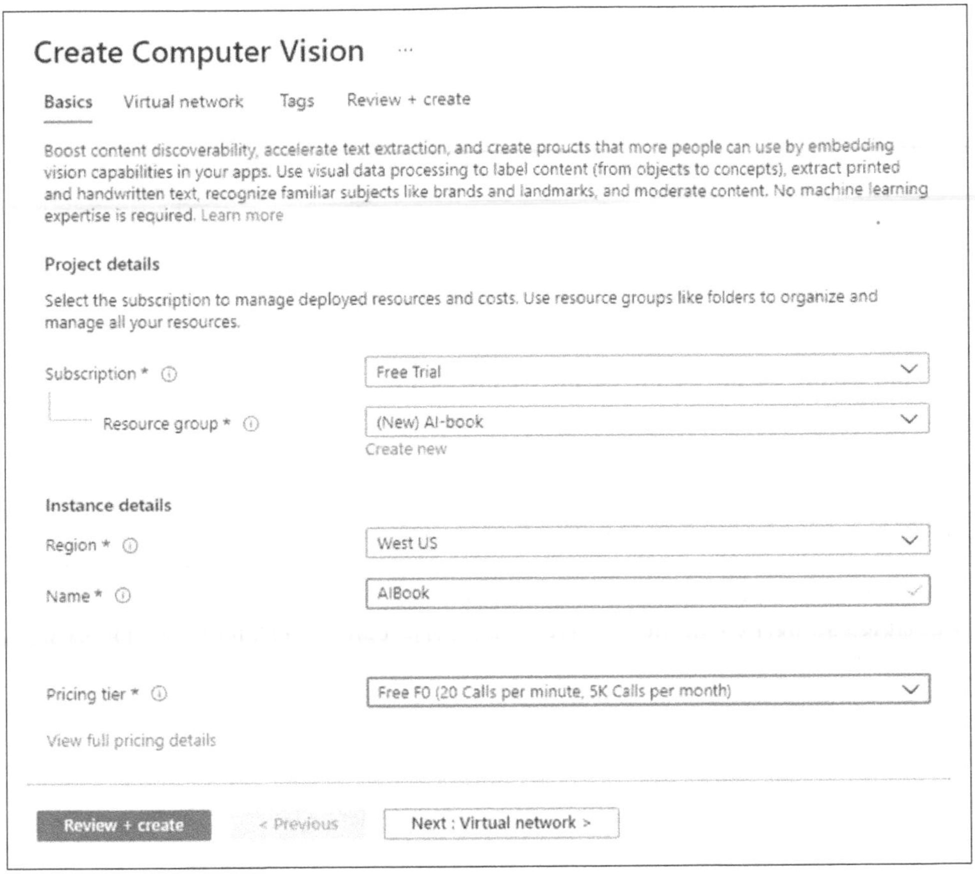

Figure 6-14. Create your Computer Vision resource in the Azure portal

Once you have created a new Computer Vision resource in Azure, copy its authentication key (you'll find two, so use the first) and the endpoint URL. These will be needed to configure the Computer Vision connector.

Go back to Power Automate and add the keys and endpoint URL before choosing Detect Objects. This will return a tag associated with the uploaded image. In the connector, choose an Image Source and Image Content, linked to the filename of the uploaded image that's extracted by the flow trigger (see Figure 6-15).

Figure 6-15. Use the filename to select new images to recognize

After configured is complete, add a final connector to send an email message to a predefined address containing the recognized object and a file handle: see Figure 6-16 for the different options you have here.

Use the Flow Checker to ensure that the basic structure of your AI-powered flow is correct and run a test to see if it works. You can click through each step in a run to see how your flow performed, with the option of seeing the data returned from the Azure Computer Vision service, including any confidence levels and alternate object detections.

The same process can be used to create more complex flows, integrating Cognitive Services with other applications via triggers and connectors, making it part of your process automation tooling.

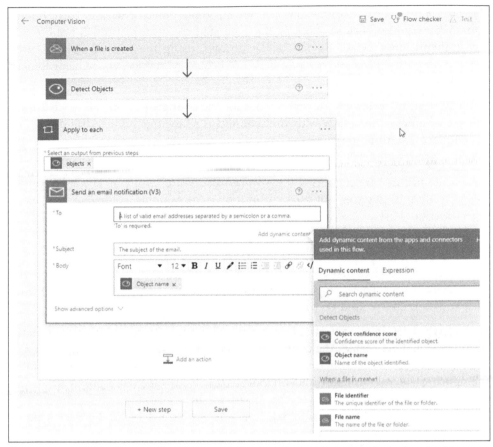

Figure 6-16. Fill in the email address and choose what metadata to include—just the object that Computer Vision detects, or details like how likely the identification is

Custom connectors

If you can't find a prebuilt connector for a service, or if you want to use a custom AI model, you can use a custom connector to call an API (note that this requires a premium subscription to Power Apps). Power Automate, Power Apps, and Logic Apps all share the same custom connector model. You'll need to work with either an OpenAPI or Postman definition of your API, or work from the Power Platform's custom connector portal. Custom connectors made using the portal are available only within the Power Platform.

To create a new custom connector, open the custom connector wizard. Next, import your API definition, before checking the generated connector. You will need to add any authentication details as part of the process, using the correct authentication method for your API. If you're using an Azure-hosted AI service, you're likely to need its API key.

You will need to review the overall settings for the connector, controlling what users can see when creating a flow with your connector. Once that's done, drill down into the connector settings to review the request and response sections. Here you'll see the data that's sent to the API along with expected returns from a successful operation.

Once the custom connector is ready, you can use Power Apps or Power Automate to test it. Simpler services can use built-in tools—for example, calling an API via an HTTP webhook.

Using Cognitive Services in Power Apps

If you need AI services that aren't available in AI Builder, Power Apps integrates with Cognitive Services. Power Apps supports the same connectors as Power Automate for this; however, they're used very differently.

If you haven't set up one yet, start by creating a Cognitive Services API account in the Azure portal. This enables the connectors in Power Apps, and you will find them in the Data section of the design tool. Search for the service you intend to use, adding the appropriate Account Key and Endpoint URL from the Azure portal when you add the connector to your Power App. If you've already configured a connection in another Power App or Power Automate flow, you won't need to add this data again.

Once added, your Cognitive Service API connector is treated as a data source, and it integrates with other data sources in your Power App. There's no need to write code to handle data translation; the platform handles this automatically for you.

You build Power Apps in the online studio, which you can access from the Power Apps website. This is a custom development environment, with support for drag-and-drop control layout as well as attaching formulas and actions to controls you've added to the application canvas. Two canvas options are available: mobile, for phones, and tablet, which also works for applications run from the web. Tablet and mobile apps can be run from the iOS and Android Power Apps applications.

Build your application UI by choosing controls from the Insert menu. This adds them to the studio canvas, where you can customize the look and feel and add actions to controls. For example, a button has an OnSelect action, while a Gallery will connect to a data source, which can be a connector (as shown in Figure 6-17), a database, a SharePoint list, or a Power Apps collection.

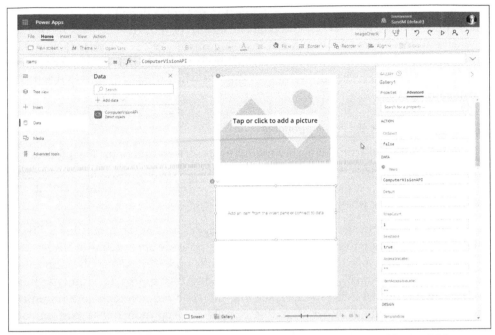

Figure 6-17. Adding a connector for the Cognitive Services Computer Vision API to a Power App

Once you have laid out your app and added a connector to a Cognitive Service, you can start to add application logic using formulas attached to control properties. These can be quite complex pieces of code, especially if you are trying to run several API functions at the same time—for example, in a customer service application that takes key phrases from a document while also detecting sentiment.

Working with Cognitive Services in Power Apps canvas apps requires some knowledge of the Power Apps formula language, Power Fx (which is also what's used in the formula bar). It's closely related to the familiar tools in Excel, with expressions starting with =, but Power Fx also incorporates some elements of SQL to cover data scenarios Excel functions don't handle, with control descriptions that owe a lot to .NET's XAML GUI environment. And (unlike Excel) it has imperative programming commands that can respond to user input and affect state. If you've built any applications in Excel or used LAMBDA and LET functions to create formulas, you shouldn't find working with it too much of a learning curve, and if you're creating your own machine learning models in Azure Machine Learning you can reference them in Power Apps from any control using Power Fx.

To simplify working with data from a connector, use collections to hold results. The ClearCollect function will create and populate a collection or reset an existing one for new data. ClearCollect will wrap a call to a Cognitive Services connector using data from application fields or from other data sources (including external data sources and other collections). The connector calls the API when triggered, storing results for use in your application.

Combining Power Apps and Power Automate

A Power App is a collection of asynchronous event-driven functions. Each formula is triggered either by an action on a control or from a data source. Your output fields will be connected to a data source that holds the results of an action, and it will automatically update when the action runs.

If you prefer, you can use a Power App as a trigger and an endpoint for a Power Automate flow. This approach allows you to use a no-code approach to working with Cognitive Services, while using Power Apps to build a user-friendly application front-end for PC (via the web), phone, and tablet. Using this approach, prototype flows can quickly be turned into products, keeping the code requirements to a minimum and giving the option of either migrating to a Power App model or to custom code without changing the user experience.

Working with a flow in this way can also offer a workaround for some Power App limitations. For example, it can provide a quick way to save and convert camera captures and use them with the Computer Vision API. The bitmaps generated from the Power App camera control need to be converted to a supported format before they can be used, and a flow can take care of that.

Logic Apps and AI

At first glance, Azure Logic Apps and Power Automate appear similar. Like Power Automate, Logic Apps is a business application integration tool designed to automate common workflows, linking different application APIs via a low-code visual programming environment. It even offers many of the same connectors. But that's where the similarities end, as Logic Apps is more akin to Microsoft's original workflow integration tool BizTalk and has been designed to work with Azure's serverless Functions and its growing suite of message-based application development tools, like Event Grid.

Message-based programming models have a long history, making them a crucial element in any distributed programming environment like Azure. Message queues help manage connections, ensuring consistency and maintaining processing order. That makes them an ideal model for building application workflows, passing data from connector to connector, and modifying message content where necessary, and they have developed into an important element in Microsoft's Azure IoT tooling.

Technologies like the CloudEvents standard and the publish and subscribe Event Grid provide a framework for managing messages and for triggering event-driven applications.

Azure Logic Apps are an important part of this approach, providing a quick way of building those connections, adding workflow and basic processing to respond to events, and triggering actions in other applications. Machine learning has a significant role to play in this scenario, adding smart filters to complex data flows or improving the quality of application inputs. By using a predictive model to identify significant data, a Logic App can quickly launch alerts or even trigger remedial action.

As it builds on the Azure serverless and event-driven platform, Logic Apps has become an important integration tool that can mix Azure services with external APIs and with your own code. Using no- and low-code techniques, Logic Apps can bring together API connectors and messages, using Functions to add snippets of custom code where necessary. When used with Azure edge and IoT tools, they also become an effective way of linking signals from the edge of a network to large-scale compute in the public cloud.

Additionally, connectors into the Azure management tooling mean that Logic Apps can also be used as a way of automating application and service management, responding to signals from applications and services, and modifying and provisioning resources in response. You can also use Logic Apps inside secure Azure networks, using an integration service environment to isolate your Logic App from the global platform.

Microsoft provides a selection of Cognitive Services connectors for Logic Apps, building on a similar connector model to Power Automate. The relevant Logic Apps connectors are:

- Computer Vision
- Content Moderator
- Custom Vision
- Face API
- Form Recognizer
- LUIS
- Microsoft Translator V2
- QnA Maker
- Text Analytics
- Video Indexer V2

You can find a list of connectors in the Logic Apps documentation. The prebuilt connectors provide a quick way of building basic machine learning–powered applications, especially around text and computer vision. These are all services that don't require real-time operations and easily can be used in flow-based applications.

While they don't cover all the possible Cognitive Services, you can use custom connectors to work with the REST APIs for other services and custom machine learning models developed using Azure's machine learning tools.

To use Cognitive Services in Azure Logic Apps, start with a subscription that contains a resource group that's connected to the Cognitive Services APIs you want to use. You can then create a new Logic App in the same resource group. This opens the Logic Apps Designer, a web-based graphical tool for choosing and configuring triggers and connectors. Start with a connector that brings in the data you want to use in your Logic App. This might be an uploaded file for computer vision or a HTTP connection with a JSON document for text analytics, or even a connection to the output of another application.

The site makes it easy to pick connectors, with Azure making suggestions about what you might want to use based on previous interactions. Start with your flow trigger—for example, uploading a file to an Azure storage blog, or updating a record in a database.

Once you have an event source to use as a trigger, you will build your Logic App flow, adding basic flow logic, before adding a connector for your chosen Cognitive Service. You'll need to configure the connector, using data from your service subscription. First add a name, then your Cognitive Services Account Key and the URL of the service endpoint your application will use. These can be found in the Azure portal and can be copied into the connector configuration.

With the connection details configured, click Create to build your Cognitive Services connector. You can now build the rest of your application, adding new steps from the service output. So, for example, if you're using a Logic App to detect user sentiment in help desk queries, your app can pass all messages that have a negative sentiment to a database, ready for additional prioritization. In this case you're using a Logic App and Cognitive Services to filter events; other applications might work with other types of trigger and other types of data.

Logic Apps are an ideal tool for quickly bringing several Azure services together, making it possible to prototype more complex applications or to quickly build a solution for an urgent problem without requiring significant development resources. Much of the code you might need to write is already part of the service, as Logic App connectors are built on top of Azure internal APIs that provide the signals needed to trigger actions and flows; so, for example, there's no need to write code to monitor file systems for changes, as any changes can be used to trigger a Logic App.

Azure service integration in Logic Apps also positions them as a system administration tool, which can help with running applications at scale by providing smart and proactive filters on logging data, using predictive machine learning models to manage Azure deployments. For example, a VM showing a certain pattern of errors, that a machine learning model uses to predict a failure, could trigger failover to another instance, followed by either a reboot or a fresh deployment of a replacement image. By working off machine learning–based predictions, application downtime is kept to a minimum, and users remain unaware of issues. This will require using a custom connector, as well as working with tools like Azure's automated machine learning training.

If you're using a custom machine learning model with Logic Apps, you'll need to create an HTTP connector to send a query to the service. Microsoft's tools make it easy to construct a REST connection, using a POST to send queries to the machine learning API endpoint. There's no need to construct the call's JSON; that's all handled by the Logic App connector using the API schema. You can get the endpoint URL and any required keys from the Azure Machine Learning tooling. It's worth using an API test tool like Postman to try out any APIs before you add them to a Logic App flow, using the resulting details to ensure that you're sending the right query data.

Custom calls will require using a Logic App connector to parse the returned JSON, working with a known schema to set flow variables that can be used to drive the rest of your application. Parsed data can be written to databases or used to construct messages that can be passed to other applications or to serverless Functions.

While the built-in Cognitive Services tooling in Logic Apps simplifies working with a subset of Azure's machine learning features, HTTP API support extends things further. You can work with your own machine learning models, newer Cognitive Services that don't yet have a connector, or with technologies like Azure AutoML. Some knowledge of JSON is essential in these cases, where you need to parse schema and work with API payloads.

One advantage of Logic Apps is that they're a low-cost option for building machine learning applications. Each action and connector is priced at fractions of a cent, with Enterprise licensed connectors costing more than standard connectors. Most Azure Machine Learning–based connectors are in the standard price band, so if you're building a relatively simple machine learning application, perhaps as part of a call center workflow, you may well end up spending only a few cents a day.

Like Power Apps and Power Automate, the Logic Apps serverless approach removes much of the risk associated with building machine learning–powered applications. Combined with a low-code approach that requires minimal training, the result is a platform that makes it easy to fill gaps in your application portfolio at the same time as assisting internal teams to build their own tools where necessary. Even so, if you want to take advantage of many of the key features of Logic Apps, some programming experience is necessary, especially if you're using it as an integration tool and need to work with REST APIs.

 Microsoft's Azure Percept industrial IoT hardware offers a low-code development environment for Computer Vision and Computer Audio services, based on Logic Apps and running in a local container on the device. You can select prebuilt models in the Percept Studio web app and deploy them directly to the AI-accelerated Percept hardware, managing them through Azure IoT Hub.

Wrapping It Up

In this chapter we looked at how you can use Microsoft's machine learning tools with its low-code and no-code platforms. By bringing together managed endpoints with simple connectors, you're able to pick and choose the features you want without needing advanced programming skills. Microsoft is taking things further still with a focus on solutions—as shown by AI Builder's prebuilt models and the option of a targeted document automation solution.

Even with tools like these, you still have to think about the impact of using AI on your users, customers, and other people who are affected by the system. In the next chapter, we will look at tools and techniques for responsible AI that can help you achieve the best outcomes and often performance too.

## CHAPTER 7

Responsible AI Development and Use

In the previous chapters, we've looked at how to use the key Microsoft cloud AI services. But it's also important to think about the bigger picture of how you build and use AI, so that you can take advantage of these cloud AI services without running into problems.

AI and machine learning are powerful techniques that can make software more useful, systems more efficient, and people more productive. But they can also violate privacy, create security problems, replicate and amplify bias, automate decision making that has negative consequences for individuals or entire groups—or just be plain wrong on occasion.

 This is a big and complicated topic, and you don't have to master every nuance to use cloud AI services. Don't get overwhelmed by all the issues: you don't need to do everything—but equally, don't assume that you don't need to do anything about responsible AI.

The greater the potential of AI—like diagnosing cancer, detecting earthquakes, predicting failures in critical infrastructure, or guiding the visually impaired through an unfamiliar location—the greater the responsibility to get it right as AI expands into areas like healthcare, education, and criminal justice, where the social implications and consequences are significant. But even everyday uses of AI could inadvertently exclude or harm users if the systems aren't fair, accountable, transparent, and secure.

Large language models like the GPT-3 model behind the Azure OpenAI Service are extremely powerful. In fact, they're so good they often sound like a human is writing the responses. But they've been trained on content both from books and many web pages, and that means that some viewpoints are heavily represented in the training data, and more marginalized perspectives are much less common or missing altogether. That means the results might be inaccurate, unfair, or downright offensive, but the language may be extremely convincing—so you need to think carefully about where to use the service and what precautions to put in place, so that you can benefit from the power it offers without exposing your users to potentially problematic responses.

As well as the social and ethical implications, there are legal issues to consider. The European Commission has proposed what's often termed the first legal framework for artificial intelligence, but the first principle of the EU General Data Protection Regulation (GDPR) already requires that personal data be processed in a fair, lawful, and transparent manner.

Too many businesses adopt AI tools without taking the time to understand that using AI without making sure that it's well managed and done ethically and fairly can have risks to the business and its reputation. One report on AI adoption in financial services,[1] where biased AI tools could wrongly exclude people from life-changing economic opportunities, showed a worrying lack of urgency around responsible AI. Two-thirds of the executives in the study couldn't explain how specific AI model decisions or predictions are made; only a fifth of the organizations had an AI ethics board or monitor models in production for fairness.

There's clearly a spectrum here: some scenarios and technologies are more straight-forward, and some are more sensitive and will require you to do more work assessing outcomes and impact.

As AI tools become more common, businesses that use AI to make decisions will need to work on keeping the trust of their customers and employees by taking on the responsibility of making sure their AI models, systems, and platforms are trustwor-thy, fair, and can be explained to the people they affect. Start by understanding the potential problems and unintended consequences, then take the risks into account as you build and test systems so they work the way you intend them to, for all your users, without discriminating against or harming them.

Remember, there are two sides to responsible AI: you need to develop your AI system responsibly, but you also need to ensure responsible use of the system, whether that's by your own employees or by your customers. And when you're consuming prebuilt cloud AI services, you need to do that responsibly as well.

For some very sensitive AI services like custom neural voice, where you're effectively duplicating a real person's voice so you can put words into their mouth, potentially in languages they don't even speak, there are specific procedures you have to follow to use the service to make sure it's not abused.

---

1 "The State of Responsible AI" (*https://go.microsoft.com/fwlink/?linkid=2190284*), FICO, May 2021.

You'll have to apply to Microsoft and be approved to use the custom neural voice service. You then have to provide Microsoft with signed releases from the person whose voice you're recording to create the neural voice to show you have informed consent, and you have to follow a code of conduct (*https://go.microsoft.com/fwlink/?linkid=2190282*) for how you use the voice. That includes always making it clear that it's a synthetic voice and even limiting what you can do with it. It might seem like a great idea to let your customers create custom messages using your celebrity voice to send a birthday greeting or make their voicemail more fun, but what if someone creates a malicious or offensive message and claims it's real?

Most cloud AI services don't have those kind of restrictions, but there may be settings where they will fail to deliver the outcome you want in ways it will be hard to avoid. That means it's helpful to go through the same kind of thought process about what your users need to know as well as what could go wrong and what policies you want to have in place to avoid or mitigate those problems.

 Being able to achieve responsible AI is more than a technical issue; there are strong cultural and organizational aspects. Understanding the impact of AI and embracing diverse perspectives so AI features work well for everyone may require some changes in mindset. It helps to get senior figures on board to make sure people and projects are accountable for results. You need to be clear about both AI and project metrics: what counts as succeeding? And if you're tackling an area where responsible AI and transparency matter, it's likely that there will be mistakes and missteps, so how the organization handles problems when they arise is important, to make sure projects get a chance to correct issues and improve.

Understanding Responsible AI

The first AI-specific regulations are still emerging, and we cover those in the next chapter, but as well as legal questions, you need to consider both ethics and performance—which aren't as separate as you might think.

There are many ways that AI can have unintended effects, and responsible AI covers a range of issues: bias, discrimination, fairness, inclusiveness, accountability, transparency, explainability, reliability and safety, privacy and security. Some of these ideas are straightforward—AI systems should perform reliably and safely, and be secure and respect privacy. Others are more complex and interconnected, so while we've broken up the tools into separate topics, you'll find a lot of overlap.

AI systems should treat all people fairly (and not knowing that an AI system will make things harder for someone doesn't stop you from being responsible if that happens). That's related to inclusivity—AI systems should empower everyone—but also to transparency and accountability. AI systems should be understandable, and people (or organizations) should be accountable for AI systems, where that means having to explain and justify decisions and actions, answer questions, and face potential consequences.

Prioritizing fairness in an AI system can mean making trade-offs with other priorities and examining assumptions, so as well as being transparent about the fact that AI is being used and what data you're collecting from users, it's important to be as transparent as possible about those priorities and assumptions.

When we talk about "explaining" AI systems, that can mean different things to different people. Machine learning experts may want to see the weights in the model that resulted in a specific prediction, as well as details of the algorithm used and dataset it was trained on, the performance scores for the model, and other technical information. That won't make things any clearer for the bank customer, who wants an explanation of why their loan was denied and what they can do about it, or for the business user who needs to understand why the system is predicting that a particular order won't be ready in time and how reliable the prediction is likely to be.

Responsible AI Improves Performance and Outcomes

Don't think about responsible AI as an ethical approach you care about only in the abstract. Putting these principles into practice is how you build and deploy a better product and achieve accurate, effective, reliable machine learning that gives you the answers you need. The benefits go far beyond compliance, and in the next chapter we'll go into more detail about how delivering responsible AI is a key part of achieving machine learning best practices.

Take transparency. It may be a legal requirement for you to be able to explain how decisions are made, including any that are automated or based on recommendations from machine learning systems. From a business perspective, you want customers to be able to trust your organization, so you need to provide transparency and you want to be clear about how decisions are being made and what impact they're having on people. Data scientists need to be able to explain models to the business team that will be using those predictions, recommendations, or other machine learning features so they're comfortable relying on them—but models that have more interpretability are also easier to debug and improve.

Experiment and Iterate

The more visibility you have into the machine learning you're using, the better results you are likely to get from it, because you understand the inputs, the context, and any limitations of the model. Machine learning is a process of experimentation, where you start with the hypothesis of how you can use data to guide a decision and look for a machine learning model that best delivers that: interpretability will help you validate that the model matches your objectives as well as being fair.

Similarly, achieving reliability means understanding the blind spots in your model so you know where it's failing and why. Thinking about the camera angles for spatial analysis as you consider privacy and sensitive locations will also help you get better accuracy. If errors in speech or image recognition are more common or more significant for specific groups of people, you may have a fairness issue—but that also suggests that your model needs more work generally.

Knowing where your data comes from and how it was collected makes it easier to know what further data you might need to improve results.

As you work to reduce errors, you need to continue to monitor error rates and where they occur to make sure you're not addressing one problem and introducing another—a debugging principle developers will be very familiar with.

Thinking about how to build an effective system involves looking at the humans involved in the system as well as the technical implementation details: that applies to AI services just as much as it does to the interface and user experience.

You need to secure your training data and your machine learning models so a competitor or malicious user can't subvert them or find ways of gaming the system (see Chapter 8 for more details on this). The specifics may be a little different, but again, starting with the same security and privacy concerns that apply to any database will help you deliver a more robust AI system.

But there are also issues you can see with AI that won't be familiar from other areas of development—and that's where responsible AI tools can help.

Tools for Delivering Responsible AI

It's important to be transparent about how you use data and apply machine learning, but you need to move beyond just transparency to make sure you operationalize the principles of responsible AI in your machine learning lifecycle. Different tools can help you to identify, diagnose, and mitigate errors, harms, and other failures of responsible AI, and help you explore data and make responsible decisions with it.

When you use cloud AI services like Cognitive Services and Azure Applied AI Services that have pretrained models or simple customization steps, many of the more operational tools won't be applicable to your workflow (though they all will have been used as part of developing the models). But the planning tools will be relevant because you still have to think about responsible AI, whether that's being transparent about the fact you're using AI services to make decisions or offer predictions, looking at the accuracy and performance results for any custom models you train, or doing thorough testing with your own data to make sure that the tools work well for your entire audience and don't exclude particular groups. If your users are likely to be taking photos outdoors, at night, or in the rain, use those kinds of images to train and test object and face recognition.

It's up to Microsoft to build the service responsibly, but it's also up to you to use it responsibly. You can't simply rely on the service always getting it right: you need to include human oversight and review of predictions, classifications, and other results—refer to "Human in the Loop Oversight" on page 153 for more details. And make sure to consult the transparency notes in the next section so you have a clear understanding of what the service can do well and any situations where it may not produce good results, and how to use it responsibly in light of that.

Some tools that help you deliver responsible AI are relevant when you're planning what you're going to build and as you evaluate ongoing projects. Others will be part of your MLOps process (turn back to Chapter 3 if you need a refresher on what that looks like in practice), so that you can train and assess models quickly and responsibly. Experimentation is a key part of successful machine learning, and if you're training your own models you'll want to train multiple models and compare them on transparency and fairness as well as on error rates and accuracy.

There are many different tools available; in this chapter we're concentrating on the various responsible AI tools available from Microsoft, which cover transparency, fairness, inclusiveness, reliability and safety, privacy, security, and accountability. Many of them are open source, but they're also integrated into services like Azure Machine Learning. You can use Microsoft's Responsible AI Toolbox (*https://aka.ms/ rai-toolbox*) to create a workflow for debugging machine learning models using the tools shown in Figure 7-1 for fairness, error analysis, and interpretability, or to do causal analysis to help you make data-driven decisions based on machine learning predictions.

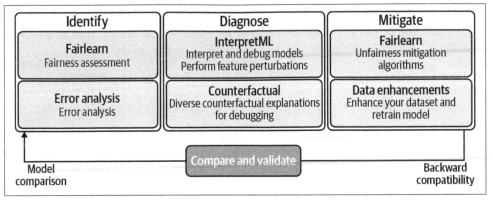

Identify	Diagnose	Mitigate
Fairlearn Fairness assessment	**InterpretML** Interpret and debug models Perform feature perturbations	**Fairlearn** Unfairness mitigation algorithms
Error analysis Error analysis	**Counterfactual** Diverse counterfactual explanations for debugging	**Data enhancements** Enhance your dataset and retrain model

Model comparison — Compare and validate — Backward compatibility

Figure 7-1. Use the tools in the Responsible AI Toolbox to create your own machine learning debugging workflow

All these tools are available separately, but the toolkit takes care of all the dependencies and wraps them in a helpful dashboard.

Tools for Transparency

Transparency isn't just about telling users that you're collecting data and using AI, or even explaining what predictions are based on, although that's important (you'll see that called explainability or interpretability). It also covers making sure developers and data scientists are clear about where data comes from so they can use it responsibly; the same applies to any prebuilt models or AI services you use.

Whether you're training your own model or customizing a pretrained one, you need to know where your training data comes from and what's in it. We'll look at how to create a responsible data culture in your organization in more detail in Chapter 8, but tracking the lifecycle of a training dataset so you know who built it and why is critical to understanding what the demographic skews might be in that set. Every dataset should be accompanied by a datasheet that documents why it was collected and how (including any processing done on it), exactly what data is contained in it (raw data or features, any confidential, sensitive, privileged, or potentially offensive data) and what's missing, its recommended uses (including any known restrictions), what it's already been used for, and so on. The Microsoft Datasheets for Datasets template (*https://go.microsoft.com/fwlink/?linkid=2190166*) includes a set of questions to help you gather the information for the datasheet.

If possible, consider the information you will need to include in the datasheet before collecting data and document the motivation, composition, collection, preprocessing, distribution, maintenance, and uses of the dataset as you go along.

Model cards and transparency notes

Even when you're using a prebuilt model or an AI service, knowing how it was built and how it works may help you use it responsibly—and effectively.

Because AI is probabilistic and statistical, it's unlikely to ever be completely accurate; understanding the limitations and where it is more likely to fail will help you design an overall system that makes better use of AI models because it takes that into account.

Model cards and transparency notes document AI models and services to help you understand their capabilities and limitations, as well as what choices you can make that influence the behavior of the system to achieve the best performance from it, like setting confidence score thresholds to minimize either false negatives or false positives, or how to preprocess data to get the best outcomes. That kind of information helps you make trade-offs and understand whether the service will work well with the kind of data you have available.

Microsoft is committed to responsible AI, and part of that is providing transparency notes and integration guidance for an increasing number of Azure AI services (see Responsible Use of AI with Cognitive Services (*https://go.microsoft.com/fwlink/?linkid=2190168*)). These tell you what kind of data will give you the best results from each service and what it will not do as well (like explaining the limitations of sentiment analysis in the Text Analytics service or warning that the OpenAI Service isn't suitable for open-ended scenarios where your users can generate content on any topic because that might produce offensive text or other undesirable but unintended responses). The documentation will tell you how to use the various Azure AI services, but the transparency notes will be especially useful for understanding what they're most suitable for.

For each of the Cognitive Services and Applied AI Services, Microsoft looks at the different fairness issues that could apply (usually it's quality of service) and tests the models used for them. So for speech-to-text, they have a test set covering age, gender, language and regional accents, plus other social factors that could cause accuracy to vary, corresponding to the real-world distribution of those in the population. As new versions of models are trained, they're tested to make sure that, in a statistically significant way and to an acceptable margin of error, they work equally well for, say, men and women. Over time, transparency notes for the different services will include the details of which factors and groups are tested for, any areas where the models are known to perform less well, and what they haven't yet been tested for, so you can compare that to your own population of users.

If the context in which you will be using a service is very different from the way Microsoft will have tested it (for example, speech recognition is usually tested in a quiet environment, and you will be using it in a noisy location where several people might be talking in the background) or you know you will be customizing the model, you will want to perform fairness assessments on your training data and model performance (we look at the tools for that later in this chapter) and keep records of those. You may also prefer to use AI in a more narrow and targeted way, limiting it to situations where you know it will perform well, experimenting with ways to expand on that once you're getting good results.

Some transparency notes also include deployment and integration guidelines with helpful information about how to use the service responsibly. That's particularly useful for emerging areas like using computer vision for spatial analysis (*https://go.micro soft.com/fwlink/?linkid=2190285*)—where you may need to balance privacy concerns with the health and safety benefits of monitoring an office or retail location to help maintain social distancing, making it even more important to make people aware what data is being collected and explain why. The details from these notes covering how your data will be processed, used, and stored by the Azure AI services may be useful to include in your own compliance records. You can create transparency notes and integration recommendations for your own models as an extension of creating datasheets for your datasets.

Checklists and planning processes for AI projects

When it comes to applying the ideas of responsible AI, it helps to have a formal process that covers areas you need to consider and decisions or trade-offs you need to make. A checklist of questions that you have to answer before processing with a project involving AI can help put that into practice. You might want to try and classify models as low, medium, or high risk. For some systems, you might want to conduct a formal algorithmic impact assessment (*https://go.microsoft.com/fwlink/?linkid=2190167*) that describes what it's designed to do and says who will be responsible for fixing any problems. When you create and work through a checklist, you're working at a higher level than dataset datasheets and transparency notes, but you're exploring the same kinds of decisions about how to design, implement, and deploy AI systems.

Microsoft offers an AI Fairness Checklist (*https://go.microsoft.com/fwlink/?linkid=2190169*) that is itself a process to work through to help you create a more specific checklist for your own situation, and despite the name, it covers a range of responsible AI topics like reliability. Use it to ask questions like:

- Who will be affected by the deployment of this system? Are there people who could be negatively affected because of this system or application being used? How could we mitigate the impact?
- What are some of the potential limitations, issues, or risks that could arise from this system?
- Will the product or feature we're planning to use perform well in our scenario? Test the AI feature on real-world data and check the accuracy before deploying.

- How will we identify and respond to error? AI services and features will rarely be 100% accurate all the time in practical use: how do we prepare for and deal with this?

- How will we measure performance and success? Specific outcomes are often better measures than usage and adoption.

Responsible AI relies on people making responsible decisions about what systems to build and thinking about the impact on those who will use or be affected by those systems.

The Human-AI eXperience (HAX) Toolkit (*https://go.microsoft.com/fwlink/? linkid=2190286*) has a set of guidelines for making those responsible decisions when you build AI systems that interact with people. For example, most people will assume that a machine learning system is always learning and will pick up on their corrections and not make the same mistake twice; but that won't happen unless you're collecting the data and retraining the model. Make it clear whether that's happening and when they might see improvements.

Use the HAX workbook to help your whole team (designers, managers, and developers) think about what the system will do and how users will interact with it before you start building. Then work through the HAX playbook to explore and plan for what can go wrong.

 Bring all of these ideas together with a structured brainstorming session. Judgement Call (*https://go.microsoft.com/fwlink/? linkid=2190170*) is a card game where your team can role-play who you think will be affected by your technology, how they will use it, what can go wrong, and what you can do about it.

Interpretability

Once you've built your machine learning model, you need to assess it. Performance matters, but it's just as important to understand as much as possible about how it works and what features in the model affect predictions and classifications. In regulated industries, interpretable models and explanations may be a legal requirement; elsewhere, stakeholders, users, and customers may have more trust in machine learning results if they can see what contributes to them—but the information may need to be presented quite differently for each audience.

Interpretability tools can help you understand which features in the data most affect the results. If you're predicting the right selling price for a house, the age of the property and ratings of local schools will usually be the most significant features in the dataset, but the size of the house and the plot it's built on, the number of bedrooms and bathrooms, whether it has a garage or a porch, and other factors like having a garden will also contribute.

The Responsible AI Toolbox has a model interpretability step powered by the open source InterpretML (*https://go.microsoft.com/fwlink/?linkid=2190287*) Python package, which can help you understand the behavior of your model generally, or the reasons for specific predictions.

The Azure Machine Learning SDK includes model interpretability classes for InterpretML in azureml.interpret that can explain model predictions by showing the distribution of predictions and how much influence specific features have on results for the whole model or for individual predictions. It has a visualization dashboard that lets you explore explanations in a Jupyter Notebook, or you can see a simplified version of the dashboard in Azure Machine Learning studio. You can try out the Azure Machine Learning Interpret APIs in these sample notebooks (*https://go.microsoft.com/fwlink/?linkid=2190171*).

As well as understanding why they didn't get a loan or why the house pricing tool suggested a particular price, a customer may also want to know what they could do to get a different result—using those machine learning predictions in the real world. If you know which features in the model were important for the prediction, you can use counterfactuals—things that aren't true but could be—to explore how the predictions would change and give them the option of exploring those suggestions, again, making it clear what they're based on.

Be careful how you present explanations of an AI system; you need to be clear that you're explaining what the model learned so that people can decide whether to trust a prediction, not describing the way the real world works. Using frequencies rather than specific numbers can also help to make it clear that predictions are probabilities rather than certainties; think about the cone of probability on a hurricane map.

The counterfactual example analysis step in the Responsible AI Toolbox, powered by InterpretML DiCE (*https://github.com/interpretml/DiCE*), lets a business user experiment with the data in a loan application that was denied to give a customer some suggestions (including saying what features can and can't be changed). It's pointless to say "be five years younger," and "earn an extra $10,000 a year" might not be immediately helpful, but being able to tell them they'll be approved if they close one of their credit cards or repay this much on an existing loan is the kind of transparency that stops AI being a black box.

But the same tool will also help you find both fairness concerns and problematic features. Models are only an approximation of the real world: they may not be accurate, and there may be correlations between features in the model that don't necessarily reflect causation in the real world. If you're looking at a model that predicts someone's income and increasing their capital loss from zero to thousands of dollars results in a higher predicted income, either there's an error in the model or it's capturing a correlation like tax strategies.

The other approach to this is asking "what if" questions to make a data-driven decision, using a causal analysis step powered by the EconML (*https://github.com/micro soft/EconML*) Python package. For our house pricing scenario, we could look at a specific house in the dataset and see how having a bigger garage or more fireplaces would change the suggested price, or get a table of houses sorted by which will see the biggest increase in price with those changes so you can focus resources on what will have the biggest impact.

You can also use this to create policies. Instead of telling everyone who wants to sell a house that adding a porch will increase the value, you can use "what if" questions to establish that an older house on a small lot will sell for a higher price if you remove an existing porch but a newer house with the main floor over a certain number of square feet will sell for more money if you add a porch.

If you want to do more advanced causal inferencing, the DoWhy Python library (*https://github.com/Microsoft/dowhy*) is also part of the Responsible AI Toolbox; it can help you model the assumptions you're making (specifying what you do and don't know) and then test them.

If you aren't familiar with causal inference, ShowWhy (*https://github.com/micro soft/showwhy*) will help you ask questions, expose assumptions, and explore causes and confounders—variables that contribute to both what you think is the cause and the final outcome—with diagrams that show the relationships in your data.

Tools for AI Fairness

AI systems can behave unfairly because of bias in society that's reflected in the training data, because of decisions made during development and deployment, or because there are flaws in the data (like not being representative of all your users) or in the system itself.

AI can automate bias that's sporadically present in the training set and amplify that by applying it routinely rather than selectively. It can also introduce bias, bringing a biased linkage like "men are doctors, women are nurses" when translating from a language that doesn't have gendered pronouns, turning "this person is a doctor, this person is a nurse" into "he is a doctor, she is a nurse."

You also need to think about mismatches between your data and the real world. If you assume that people who spend longer looking at a web page are more interested in that topic, you're not taking into account people who might be on a slow internet connection, or whether the page design makes it harder for some people to read.

AI fairness means assessing the possible negative outcomes a model could have on individuals or groups, and mitigating those. There are a lot of different negative impacts (often called "harms") an AI system can have, but there are three main types of fairness to think about when you look at how an AI system behaves—although a fairness problem might cause more than one kind of harm.

Quality of service fairness is about the accuracy of the system. If you train your system on data that covers one specific scenario but use it in a broader, more complex situation, it's likely to perform poorly. Facial recognition is often less accurate for people with dark skin, and especially so for women with dark skin; that's a quality of service failure because it's less accurate for one group of people. That's because the datasets facial recognition models are trained on don't have enough examples for the model to learn the right patterns.

If you have insufficient coverage in your data, you may be able to mitigate the problem by collecting more data: if not, you can look into options like synthetic data, or you can choose not to use the model in those cases. So if you use click data to train a recommendation system, there will be some groups of people who have never been shown a recommendation, so you can't get click data to train the system for them: in those cases, you can default to choosing randomly between some preset links.

Allocation fairness is about whether your AI system is offering everyone the same opportunities or resources, or if one group of people is more likely to be offered a loan or have their resume accepted by a job application system. If you have a quality of service problem with your model and you apply it to a group of people that the model is less accurate for, you could end up creating an allocation harm. Speech-to-text models that have been trained on speech in quiet settings will be less accurate in a noisy environment, but you may also find that background noise affects the performance of the model more for one group than another.

The Fairlearn tool (*https://fairlearn.org*) in the Responsible AI Toolbox will show you both the accuracy of model performance across different groups, for finding quality of service issues, and the decisions it makes so you can look for allocation harms.

Translating gender-neutral language as "he is a doctor, she is a nurse" is stereotyping, but it's also an example of what's called representational harm. If a particular group is systematically under- or overrepresented, it can suggest that they don't belong in that profession or situation, like an image search for CEOs that returns pictures only of men. Image tagging and captioning can produce an image and caption that would be acceptable separately, but the juxtaposition can be problematic.

Not all failures are equal. If your system produces an image caption that looks like it's reinforcing harmful or historical stereotypes, that can be more of a problem for your users than a caption that just doesn't make sense, even though they may both look like errors when you measure the accuracy of your model.

InterpretML can help you understand the features in your model that can lead to some of these harms, as can the tools for exploring model accuracy in the next section. If you want to dive deeper into understanding the different kinds of harms, you'll find more information at the end of this chapter.

Tools for Reliability and Understanding Error

Reliability is about understanding the blind spots of your model. Where and why is it failing?

Consider situations in which your models are less accurate rather than looking at a single performance score. If you're working with images that include pictures taken outdoors, is the visual recognition still accurate when it's dark and raining? If you're building a loan approval model, does it perform similarly for groups of applicants of different age, gender, education, or ethnicity? The Error Analysis step in the Responsible AI Toolbox can help you understand the distribution of errors by discovering which groups in your data (known as cohorts) have high error rates, investigating which input features affect those error rates, and exploring the model, features, and dataset to debug predictions.

The graphical visualization is particularly helpful here, showing error rates for specific features. You can mark the ones that look particularly interesting—or problematic—and then explore the statistics for those cohorts. Perhaps there are a lot of false negatives for certain groups; that means you'll want to look at the data distribution in the data explorer to see if it's balanced. If you have too little data for those groups it will make the model less accurate, so this can point you to what data you need to collect to improve it.

You can also look at which are the most important features the model uses to make predictions and compare those across your cohorts. Again, that gives you a better understanding of what your model has learned. You can also generate explanations—although those will make sense to a data scientist rather than an end user, so if you're going to present accuracy levels and other information about your model to the people who are interacting with it, you'll need different tools for generating those.

Human in the Loop Oversight

Concepts of fairness are complicated: they can be domain and context sensitive, and you also may need to consider long-term impacts as well as immediate harms. No automated attempt to assess fairness is going to give the same nuanced judgment as humans assessing the underlying distributions in the data, how well models represent the real world, and what impact they might have. The proposed EU regulations on development and use of AI require human oversight of "high-risk A.I. systems," and the 2020 Washington State facial recognition law mandates "meaningful human review."

But simply having a person review and rubber-stamp decisions proposed by machine learning models doesn't avoid all possible harms either; the human may have their own biases and assumptions, they may place too much trust in the automated system,[2] or they may not have enough seniority to make any meaningful changes to the outcome. Just seeing the AI prediction might affect their own decision; if you look at a transcript before hearing an audio recording, it can be hard to hear the words spoken as anything other than the words you've read—just as the caption on an optical illusion can affect how you first perceive it.

You need to consider what information will be available to the human exercising that oversight, what incentives they have to uphold or reject automated decisions, and how you can responsibly present the AI suggestions and allow the user to explore alternatives.

If you're using the Azure OpenAI Service to generate text that looks as if it's written by a human being, consider whether you need the user to know it was autogenerated rather than written and reviewed by another person. Offering multiple suggestions for users to pick from, and explicitly calling them suggestions, may avoid them just clicking OK without taking the time to consider if it's accurate and appropriate.

The OpenAI Service includes content filters that let you customize the tone and topic of the content produced. But if it's generating something critical, whether that's legal advice, contract boilerplate, or APIs to give low-code developers access to your enterprise's own data and services, you want to design a thorough review process into the workflow.

Automatic aggregations in Power BI are created by machine learning that analyzes user query patterns so the system can cache aggregate measures that will improve

---

2 Research suggests that even though we know they're not people, we instinctively treat computers as if they were (Reeves, B., and C. Nass. *The Media Equation: How People Treat Computers, Television, and New Media Like Real People and Places.* [New York: Cambridge University Press, 1996]). Helping your users create a "mental model (*https://go.microsoft.com/fwlink/?linkid=2190175*)" of how an AI system makes predictions and decisions can help them decide when they should trust those suggestions and when they should question them.

query performance without consuming too many resources. A slider allows administrators to fine-tune this behavior, so they can make their own decisions about the trade-off between performance and storage. If it's appropriate for your app, giving users the option to explore and experiment can help them make the best decision.

Make sure it's clear what the confidence values are for each prediction or decision, and build apps that support people by making information available rather than replace them. When measuring the effectiveness of AI systems, look beyond simple precision and recall metrics and look at whether they help people get better results than they would without using the system.

If you have a chatbot or an automated system, think about how you can provide an "off-ramp" to allow users to escalate their question to a human—and include the information they've already provided so they don't have to explain everything from the beginning. There may be topics that the AI could handle but that you will want to have a person deal with instead, because they're complicated or nuanced. And the more sophisticated the chatbot is—especially if you have a realistic neural voice or text that reads as if it was written by a human from the services we looked at in Chapter 4—the more important it is to be clear when someone is interacting with an AI system rather than a real person and to tell them how to reach a human instead.

Having a fallback option is key; if your user isn't happy with the automatic results from an AI tool, give them a way to fill in the details themselves or to contact a human to help them instead. Collecting examples (with permission) of where your models aren't producing good results gives you useful data for further development and training, but remember to tell the user what you will do with that data and whether they should expect to see changes.

 Your users will frequently expect the AI system to learn and get better based on how they interact with it: make it clear whether that happens or not. Asking for feedback and examples of where the system isn't working can be a good way to find beta testers for your next version. That will also help you understand which kind of failures are really important, because not all errors are the same and there are some you need to work harder to deal with (if they're offensive rather than just confusing, say).

Use the tools for transparency, interpretability, error analysis, and causal reasoning to explore what you should tell the human in the loop. For example, the HAX Toolkit has a set of guidelines for how AI systems should interact with humans, illustrated by the design library of helpful patterns shown in Figure 7-2, with examples drawn from familiar services.

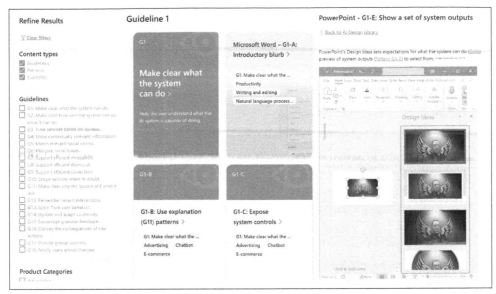

Figure 7-2. The HAX Toolkit guidelines will help you present AI features responsibly

"Human in the loop" also applies while developing machine learning models—for example, using machine learning to suggest the labels for training data that a person (ideally someone with expertise in the area) still has to accept and apply.

Wrapping It Up

In this chapter we've looked at what you can think of as the Spiderman principle: AI is powerful—and with great power comes great responsibility. Even if you're using rather than building machine learning models, it's important to think about what could go wrong and use the principles of responsible AI to avoid or mitigate potential issues. The tools we've covered will help you move from thinking about how to use AI ethically to making that part of your machine learning workflow to get the practical benefits; doing well by doing good, as it were.

But while responsible AI is where you need to start, there are other issues to consider alongside it, like experimentation and collaboration. In the next chapter we'll look at how to build a strong data culture that will help you deliver all the best practices that support responsible AI.

Further Resources

Responsible AI is a broad topic with important research still ongoing; if you want to dive in more deeply, there's a wide range of resources:

- See all Microsoft's Responsible AI principles (*https://go.microsoft.com/fwlink/?linkid=2190289*) in one place.

- Microsoft Learn: Identify principles and practices for responsible AI (*https://go.microsoft.com/fwlink/?linkid=2190290*) covers setting up a governance model and applying responsible AI practices in your organization.

- If you're a manager or business executive managing people who build AI systems for your organizations, take a look at the Ten Guidelines for Product Leaders to Implement AI Responsibly (*https://go.microsoft.com/fwlink/?linkid=2190291*), a guide written by Microsoft and Boston Consulting Group.

- If you want to explore AI checklists further, the BBC's Machine Learning Engine Principles (*https://go.microsoft.com/fwlink/?linkid=2190292*) includes a useful example, although some of the questions are very specific to dealing with content and broadcasting. For healthcare, the Transparent Reporting of a multivariable prediction model for Individual Prognosis Or Diagnosis (TRIPOD) Initiative (*https://www.tripod-statement.org*) has a detailed checklist for developing prediction models, which gives a good idea of the level of detail necessary for transparency in a regulated industry. For organizations affected by the GDPR, the Information Commissioner's Office's (ICO's) AI and Data Protection Risk Toolkit (*https://go.microsoft.com/fwlink/?linkid=2190294*) focuses on compliance but includes a comprehensive list of risks, including fairness, transparency, and meaningful human review as well as security and accountability, with practical steps for addressing each risk.

- ICO Guidance on ensuring lawfulness, fairness, and transparency in AI systems (*https://go.microsoft.com/fwlink/?linkid=2190179*)

- Azure Cloud Advocates Machine Learning for Beginners: Fairness in Machine Learning (*https://go.microsoft.com/fwlink/?linkid=2190296*).

- Explore different kinds of AI harms and fairness issues and learn how to assess which might occur with your system with Harms Modeling (*https://go.microsoft.com/fwlink/?linkid=2190178*).

- See the impact of a common representational harm with Gender Shades (*http://gendershades.org*), a site that lets you explore a seminal paper on responsible AI in facial recognition, and see what happened after it was published in the Coded Bias (*https://www.codedbias.com*) documentary.

- "Unfairness by Algorithm: Distilling the Harms of Automated Decision-Making." (*https://go.microsoft.com/fwlink/?linkid=2190297*) The Future of Privacy Forum has a comprehensive taxonomy of the problems that can be caused by "algorithmic discrimination," along with suggested strategies.

- The Algorithmic Impact Assessment report (*https://go.microsoft.com/fwlink/?linkid=2190298*) looks at how to evaluate approaches to responsible AI and accountability.

## CHAPTER 8

Best Practices for Machine Learning Projects

Delivering the responsible AI outcomes we discussed in the previous chapter means setting and implementing machine learning best practices. Because machine learning and AI techniques draw on data science, with a strong focus on practical outcomes, good data handling is critical. Before you develop best practices for machine learning specifically, you also need to think about how to have a data culture in your organization—a set of norms and behavior that encourages basing decisions on data—for those best practices to build on.

Working Well with Data

A data culture requires widespread data literacy. People need to understand how to work responsibly with data and have the tools to access, manipulate, prepare, and visualize data. Some of this is about technical systems you put in place, but as the term suggests, some of it is social and cultural issues. With on-demand, cloud AI tools, it's especially easy to think that gathering and curating data responsibly is "someone else's problem," but working responsibly with data is both an individual and collective responsibility across the organization.

Everyone should be asking key questions about data:

- What is the value of this data? Did we need to collect it, and should we keep it?

- What did we collect this data for, and what can we use it for?

- What are we doing with this data, how are we telling users about that, and what control do we give them?

- How is this data protected?

Sharing Data

Data silos and fragmentation of data between departments and different tools (maybe with proprietary formats) leave you with pockets of data that can't be integrated. Putting a data platform in place makes it easier to access and use all the data you have, and using cloud data storage can simplify that. For example, data from Azure Blob storage that's part of a Power BI dataflow is stored in Dataverse and accessible to Azure Data Factory, Azure Databricks, Azure Notebooks, and other services so it can be shared and reused (with the appropriate access and permissions).

Encourage people to share data and build data quality and curation processes so there aren't multiple, slightly different versions of the same dataset in different teams and data stores.

Data sharing between colleagues and across teams means rather than different teams doing the same data preparation on the same data, people can build on each other's work, improving on and standardizing data artifacts and contributing their own expertise to the process. They do that in the tools they're comfortable with. So, a business analyst would explore a dataset in Power BI to understand historical patterns, and a data engineer might use the same dataset as machine learning training data in Azure Machine Learning to use those patterns for predictions and scoring new deals. Power BI dataflows can be used in multiple reports by colleagues but also enriched by developers using other tools like Azure Databricks.

Sharing and reusing data artifacts also enables more rigorous data classification, data governance, and lifecycle management.

Data Provenance and Governance

Governance of your machine learning practices matters for both business and performance reasons. If you don't have the right framework and processes in place for handling data responsibly—assessing bias, fairness, explainability, and the other fundamentals we covered in the previous chapter—as well as privacy and security, the robustness and long-term performance of your models are likely to be poor. Without those processes, you can't track and measure the impact of changes to your data and your model as you experiment and iterate.

Understanding the provenance of datasets is important for using them responsibly. That can be a legal requirement under regulations like the GDPR and the California Consumer Privacy Act, but even without regulation, data collected under one set of circumstances may simply not be useful for or relevant in different circumstances.

Physical or external systems may change over time, sensors may be moved to different locations, and different collection methods can skew physical readings. For data about people, the demographics of the audience or the economic conditions might have changed or not be representative of your own users and audience. Survey data from a different field might use different terminology or definitions for the same term. Even common terms can have different meanings in different regions and geographies: a biscuit is a very different thing in the United Kingdom and the United States!

Curating labels

You need to assess the quality of crowd-sourced labels, captions, and tags in training data, thinking about both accuracy and possible cultural bias. Have a clear policy for handling labeling you do yourself, and provide a consistent set of labels for people to choose from, with examples and definitions to work from. Create clear guidelines on how confident you want someone to be about the labels they choose, what they should do if multiple labels seem appropriate or no labels fit, and how to make changes if they realize they made a mistake on a label.

For images, you may want to use the Azure Machine Learning ML-assisted labeling feature, which takes the manual label done on an image dataset and uses it to cluster images to speed up tagging, and then predicts labels and bounding boxes around objects that you can accept or change. This helps with both the time it takes to label data and the consistency of the labels.

Using a portable format like COCO (*https://cocodataset.org*) for labeled datasets helps with dataset sharing (and tools like Roboflow (*https://roboflow.com/formats/coco-json*) can convert to and from other formats).

Datasets need to be labeled with the details of how, when, and where the data was collected, as well as why it was collected—both the legal basis and the original purpose it was collected for, because that can have implications for how comprehensive the data is. More data doesn't automatically improve performance: having the right data matters more than having "big data" and just hoping the data you need is in there. Especially for training custom versions of existing models, having the relevant data well labeled will improve performance far more than large amounts of data that hasn't been carefully curated.

Consider what's in your data

Data minimization—collecting only what you really need—is also an important principle for compliance. It may mean that a dataset you expect to contain the data you need may not actually include it because it was collected for a different purpose. The answer to that isn't to cast a wider net and collect more data without knowing if it's relevant. As the ICO, the UK's data protection regulator, has stated, "finding the correlation does not retrospectively justify obtaining the data."

The datasheets template from Chapter 7 will help here. If you use a data governance tool like Azure Purview for classifying and understanding what data you have, this can also work against structured datasets.

You also need to document your data preparation pipeline and any data transformation or enrichment that's performed as part of it. That data lineage is important for experimentation: the data preparation needs to be consistent and repeatable so you can compare the performance and accuracy of different versions of a model. Services like Azure Machine Learning offer automated auditing of lineage through a model registry, in the same way they track the results of machine learning experiments and where datasets and models are used.

If you're working with data that contains personal or sensitive information (where encryption at rest isn't sufficient and you need to protect it during processing), you may need to de-identify and anonymize some of the information using techniques like data masking, pseudonymization, and aggregation, as well as creating legal and organizational safeguards like access controls, usage policies, and segregation of personal data from more general data. You'll also need to assess the risk of re-identification if the data is combined with other publicly available information. Or you might need to look into emerging techniques like differential privacy that inject noise to prevent that kind of correlation using tools like SmartNoise (*https://go.microsoft.com/fwlink/?linkid=2190181*), or homomorphic encryption for machine learning on encrypted data (*https://go.microsoft.com/fwlink/?linkid=2190182*).

Compliance and audit

The data you use for machine learning will likely fall under your organization's compliance policies. At the very least, you may need to document the reproducibility and auditability of machine learning systems. Using a cloud AI service can simplify this, because you can extract details like model versioning and usage, for your own models, and refer to compliance documentation for the service for prebuilt models and APIs that you consume.

For regulated industries and in jurisdictions with privacy regulations, you may want to seek professional advice on whether your organization counts as a data controller or data processor when doing machine learning and what that will mean for compliance policies. As well as data collection, you need to consider data protection principles including accountability and privacy-by-design requirements. If you're using machine learning for automated decision making or profiling, you may need to assess privacy, data protection, and compliance risks formally.

Security for machine learning

You also need to think about the security of training and operational data and securing access to the machine learning system in operation. You need to balance giving enough people access to datasets and machine learning resources to get value from them with adhering to security and compliance policies. The premise of machine learning is that you don't know before you explore the data what insights you will be able to find in it, because training a machine learning model is how you discover what features in the data deliver the best predictions.

Using cloud AI services can make compliance much easier because the cloud service handles more of that, although you need to secure the accounts and credentials you use. Use RBAC and principles of least privilege; not everyone should have access to every dataset. Someone with access for labeling data shouldn't necessarily be able to delete data or use it to train a model.

 Use virtual networks and Azure Private Link to ensure you can connect to your Azure Machine Learning workspace only from a set of private IP addresses on a virtual network rather than any public IP address (and remember to move your storage and inferencing environment onto the same VNet).

Like any other computing system, a machine learning system can have security vulnerabilities: in machine learning libraries, in training, in inference, or in the deployment of the model.

You have the same kind of shared responsibility model with cloud AI services as with other cloud services. The cloud AI service takes care of vulnerabilities in machine learning libraries by patching and updating regularly. Abusing deployment vulnerabilities requires write access to change a machine learning model (although read access could allow an attacker to steal a model, assess it offline, and use what they learn to attack your model in use). Either way, you need to limit and secure access to the cloud AI service by using RBAC and protecting credentials for the service and the model. The versioning and usage information in the cloud service will again be useful for auditing this.

Vulnerabilities in training can be handled by validating input and doing integrity checks on your datasets. Vulnerabilities in inferencing are usually attackers trying to fool the machine learning model by crafting input that isn't what it appears to be (putting strips of tape on a stop sign so it's recognized as a speed limit sign instead), but it could also be input that's in an unexpected context: like a shop sign in the form of a stop sign or temporary traffic lights on the back of a truck driving in front of your car.

These "adversarial" attacks are harder to protect against; think about how your machine learning model could be attacked and use adversarial examples in training, or limit the number of inferencing calls that can be made to the model by any one source to prevent someone from sending hundreds of messages to figure out what will or won't get through.

Security professionals can use Microsoft's open source Counterfit tool (*https://github.com/Azure/counterfit*) to automate security risk assessments of AI models hosted locally or in the cloud using adversarial AI frameworks, using approaches they will be familiar with, without needing to become machine learning experts themselves. The datasheets and transparency notes we looked at in the previous chapter will also be useful for the inventory of machine learning systems they will need to conduct.

Use the AI Security Risk Assessment Framework (*https://go.microsoft.com/fwlink/?linkid=2190302*) to guide you in securing your machine learning systems in ways that build on the security risk assessment you already do in other areas of development and operations. There's a comprehensive guide to threat modeling AI and machine learning systems (*https://go.microsoft.com/fwlink/?linkid=2190183*) that will help you walk through assessing, testing, and improving your systems. If you're just starting to think about machine learning security, the defensive guidelines for Counterfit (*https://go.microsoft.com/fwlink/?linkid=2190301*) are a good place to start even if you're not using the tool.

Don't forget to think about when dataset and machine learning models will be retired and replaced. Consider policies for how long data will stay relevant, how to assess if it's out of date, and how to assess the long-term quality of predictions as a model ages.

With data governance and sharing in place, you can start to build a process that will make you more likely to get useful outcomes from machine learning.

Making Machine Learning Projects Successful

The point of doing machine learning and other forms of AI is to help solve problems; that means you need to know what problem you're trying to help solve with a particular machine learning project.

In addition to having the right process for handling data, you need clear guidelines for how you use machine learning to drive decisions. These should start by exploring and documenting the problem: what's the question the machine learning model needs to answer, and what is the decision or action that needs to be taken that can be informed by data. If you're not solving your own problem, you need to spend time with the business team who will be using the answers from the machine learning system to understand the issues. You may want to have a domain expert involved in the specification, testing, and validation.

Start by solving the problem manually, or by using heuristics; that will make sure you have a clear understanding of the problem and of the data that's available. This will also give you a baseline for measuring the success of your machine learning improvements against (and if using machine learning doesn't give better results than solving the problem manually, think carefully about whether machine learning is really applicable).

Then you can map the business scenario to a data science question that you can apply machine learning to; use the examples in Table 8-1 to help you frame your own list of scenarios, decisions, and questions.

Table 8-1. Real-world scenarios mapping business problems to data science questions

Business scenario	Key decision	Data science question
Predictive maintenance	Should I service this piece of equipment?	What is the probability this equipment will fail within the next x days?
Energy forecasting	Should I buy or sell energy contracts?	What will be the long-/short-term demand for energy in a region?
Customer churn	Which customers should I prioritize to reduce churn?	What is the probability of churn within x days for each customer?
Personalized marketing	What product should I offer first?	What is the probability that customers will purchase each product?
Product feedback	Which service/product needs attention?	What is the social media sentiment for each service/product?
Root cause analysis	Why is this product out of stock?	What are the key influencers for stock levels for each product and distribution center?

Preparing Your Dataset

You need a "balanced" dataset with enough examples of the different categories of data and a balanced distribution. If you're teaching a custom image recognizer to detect different products from your catalog or different kinds of damage to those products, you need examples of all of them with photos taken in different situations, at different times of day, in different lighting conditions, from different distances, and roughly similar numbers of images for each type, like the second set of photos in Figure 8-1.

Imagine you're teaching an image recognizer the difference between roses and daisies. If all the pictures of the daisies are closeups of the flower and all the pictures of roses are pictures of the whole rose bush, a close-up picture of a white rose is more likely to be misrecognized as a daisy. It's very common for healthcare AI systems, trained with images designed to teach human doctors, to learn to recognize not the condition shown in those photos but the ruler included for scale!

 If you're using Azure Machine Learning AutoML, it performs several optimizations to avoid overfitting and shows charts and metrics to help you identify if your data is unbalanced.

Figure 8-1. Use the top set of training images and you'll accidentally train a model that knows the difference between fruit on a plate and fruit someone is holding rather than apples and oranges: the lower set of training images is more diverse and balanced

In the real world, the distribution of types and categories is often not even or balanced. If you're training an image recognition system to detect when a traffic light is red, green, or yellow, you're going to have a lot more images of red and green traffic lights because traffic lights are either red or green for much longer than they're yellow. With a representative real-world dataset, the model will learn only the dominant classes—and it can show strong accuracy without ever learning to recognize yellow traffic lights because they're comparatively rare.

That means you need to balance the training dataset so it has more equal numbers of all three traffic light states, probably with some close-up images that show the traffic lights without the background of the road and traffic, so the system isn't learning the state of traffic flow rather than the state of the traffic lights. (It can be hard to get examples of underrepresented data, and you may have to look into using synthetic data.)

It's important to split your training data and reserve part of the dataset for validation, and a separate portion for testing. It's also important not to adjust the training and test sets so that the model performs better on the test dataset, because that makes the model vulnerable to overfitting: where the model fits the training data so well it fails on real-world data because it hasn't learned the general patterns that allow it to work with new data. Take the time to build a test set with data that represents what the model will need to deal with in use.

To avoid overfitting, you can use cross-validation—splitting your data into different subsets and training a model on each. This also avoids the temptation to tweak the training set to get a better score, but the process will take longer because you're training the model multiple times rather than just once, so you'll usually have to choose that explicitly. Again, it's important to document all these decisions.

Establish Performance Metrics

Like any other kind of development, once you know what problem you need to solve with machine learning, you need to document what success will look like, so the project makes progress toward the right goal. Again, make sure the business users are involved here.

There are quite a few metrics to choose from for scoring the success of predictions; cloud AI services will automatically show you many of these for a model.

When scoring the accuracy of a model, consider not just how many times the model gets the right answer (correctly identifying the color of the traffic light), which is the precision score, but also what's known as recall: how many images of yellow traffic lights are correctly recognized rather than being marked as red or green? Figure 8-2 shows how those scores are calculated.

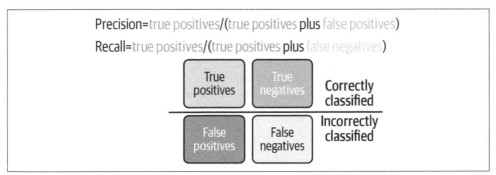

Figure 8-2. Precision and recall measure how often the model is right and which predictions the model is right about

There are other accuracy metrics that are useful for specific machine learning algorithms. One of the most commonly used metrics for regression tasks is *root-mean-square error* (RMSE). This is defined as the square root of the average squared distance between the actual score and the predicted score, as shown here:

$$\text{RMSE} = \sqrt{\frac{1}{n}\sum_{j=1}^{n}\left(y_j - \hat{y}_j\right)^2}$$

Here, y_j denotes the true value for the ith data point, and $\hat{y}_j$ denotes the predicted value. One intuitive way to understand this formula is that it is the Euclidean distance between the vector of the true values and the vector of the predicted values, averaged by n, where n is the number of data points.

Also, think about the implications of a prediction or classification being wrong. Are false positives or false negatives more of a problem? Is it worse to miss an opportunity because a deal had an inaccurately low prediction of success, or to spend time on deals that don't result in a sale because they were scored too highly? These decisions are even more significant if you might be excluding or penalizing people, so you need to work through the responsible AI principles we looked at in the previous chapter as you decide what models provide good enough results to use.

 Measuring the accuracy of results from the OpenAI Service is a more open-ended question because it depends on both the business outcome you're trying to achieve and the nuance and complexity of the task you're giving it. You'll usually start by using the "few-shot" approach of giving just a few examples as a proof of concept to see if the service is a good fit and then fine-tuning the model with further prompts and completion examples. By design, you'll get different results from the OpenAI API every time you send the same prompt, and you can use the temperature parameters to control how much variation you get in the responses. Choosing between two suggested paragraphs of text is often a very subjective decision, so you need to think about how to quantify "accuracy" and "suitability" for your specific problem, and you need to consider safety as well as accuracy (for example, are the responses generated appropriate for the context you're using them in, and are you presenting them with the right level of transparency). Some responses may be blank, so you'll need a way to screen those out.

Whichever accuracy metrics are relevant to your particular machine learning model, you need to connect them to the business outcomes you want to achieve. A model can be accurate without being useful if what you generate isn't helping someone make their decision or complete their task, so consider model scores in context. Sentiment analysis might detect with perfect accuracy that a customer is upset when speaking to a call center agent; if that's because they're calling to cancel the subscription of a family member who recently died, there's nothing that the agent can do to "fix" the situation, and offering discounts or other retention incentives would be inappropriate.

Transparency and Trust

In the previous chapter we looked at how important it is to be able to understand and explain models and the decisions made using them. Your machine learning process needs to include sharing the accuracy and confidence levels of a model and explaining how it works and what it's good or bad at predicting to the people who will use it and the people who will be affected by it. That might mean presenting to a business team and other stakeholders what the metrics are for the model, including accuracy, what the confidence levels actually mean in practice, and what features the model depends on, documenting those details for customers or simply tracking them in case of an audit.

Experiment, Update, and Move On

The metrics for a model should help you understand how well it does at solving the problem and answering the question you set for it. Although you might be able to get good results from a prebuilt cloud AI service immediately, in many cases you will want to experiment with different models, different algorithm and hyperparameter choices, or—when you're customizing a model—different training datasets to see if you get better results.

Part of the good data culture we looked at earlier in the chapter is embracing experimentation and respecting the results of those experiments:

- Define hypotheses clearly but don't cling to them.
- Be willing to learn from experiments (successes and failures).
- Look at what has worked for other people.
- Share the learning with peers.
- Promote successful experiments to production.
- Understand that failure is a valid outcome of an experiment.
- Quickly move on to the next hypothesis.
- Refine the next experiment.

Track model performance over time as well as when you first create it, and look at how well it correlates with metrics like sales, revenue, customer satisfaction, and the other outcomes you care about. As circumstances change, you may need to update, retire, or replace a model: document the end of the machine learning process as well as the beginning.

Collaboration, Not Silos

Knowing when a model needs updating—or even if it's useful in the first place—means not working in isolation. The appeal of prebuilt cloud AI services and AI integration in low-code systems is that they allow business users to use machine learning to solve their own problems, but when there are developers, data engineers, or data scientists involved, they will need to collaborate with each other and with the business team that will be using the machine learning model.

Set up your machine learning process so that they all have the right tools and access to work on the areas that matter to them—ingesting and preparing data, building, deploying, and updating models for data scientists; building, maintaining, deploying, and updating the application for developers—but that they can easily work together. Cloud AI platforms like Azure Machine Learning simplify this with RBAC and integration to other systems like Power Platform: data scientists can have access to the full machine learning workspace, data engineers get access to data preparation and labeling tools, and the machine learning models can be shared with application developers and low-code business users.

Wrapping It Up

In this chapter we've looked at how putting responsible AI into your machine learning process helps you to build best practices that protect your customers and your organization and to get the best performance out of your machine learning models and datasets.

Remember that this is as much about building a responsible data culture based on widespread data literacy as about any specific techniques or tools. It's also about defining clearly what problems you're trying to solve, which means understanding the business scenario.

One advantage of cloud AI services is that it removes the need to manage the infrastructure your machine learning systems run on—or even, with Cognitive Services, the need to build those systems yourself. Want to take a peek behind the scenes of Cognitive Services to see how Microsoft puts these responsible AI principles and machine learning best practices into action, at scale? Check out the next section.

## PART III

AI-Oriented Architectures in the Real World

## CHAPTER 9

How Microsoft Runs Cognitive Services for Millions of Users

In the last two chapters, we looked at how important it is to use AI responsibly and with the best practices for machine learning that deliver a practical and responsible AI system. But what does the infrastructure and process for doing that look like in action?

The Azure Cognitive Services we covered in Chapter 4 run 24 7 in more than 30 Azure regions, underpinning features in Microsoft's own applications as well as for large organizations like Airbus, Progressive Insurance, Uber, and Vodafone, powering apps for thousands of employees and millions of their customers.

There are more than 54 billion Cognitive Services transactions a month; the Speech services alone transcribe over 18 million hours of speech a month. Decision APIs power 6 million personalized experiences on Xbox every day, and over a billion images have been captioned in PowerPoint and Word with automatic alt text created by the Vision services. As Teams usage grew during the pandemic, so did Cognitive Services usage, because it powers live captioning in meetings and transcription of recorded meetings. The Speech services had to scale sevenfold to handle Teams caption needs, which consume 2 million core hours of compute a day on Azure.

And the different Cognitive Services are updated continuously with previews, new features, and fixes to any vulnerabilities in the underlying technology stack. If you want to run your own machine learning models, or some of the Cognitive Services in containers on your own infrastructure, you have to handle all those deployments, updates, and security boundaries yourself.

That's important if you have data sovereignty issues or if you want to use AI at the edge where you don't have connectivity or need real-time decisions—on an oil rig or a factory production line.

But the models used in the Cognitive Services containers you can run have been optimized for that. If you use Azure Percept IoT devices to get AI insights at the edge, they rely on Cognitive Services, but they use tiny versions of the models that can run on a camera rather than in the powerful VMs available in the cloud.

It's also easier for a cloud service to handle bursts of traffic efficiently and economically. It's not just that a hyperscale provider like Azure will get a better deal buying hardware, network bandwidth, and electricity because they buy so much or even have the operational expertise—important as that is. If you have only one customer and they have a burst of traffic, having the capacity for that means provisioning hardware that may be underutilized the rest of the time. With thousands of customers, cloud services have a bigger buffer to handle surges in demand from any one customer, meaning it costs less to deliver that scale.

AI for Anyone

What is now Cognitive Services launched in 2015 as four APIs under the codename Project Oxford, for vision, speech, face recognition, and language understanding. Another five APIs soon followed, then another dozen, with the latest techniques and models developed by Microsoft Research moving quickly into production. But by the time there were 30 Cognitive Services, each service ran on its own instance of any of four different platforms with its own support team.

That kind of fragmentation happens as you develop new products quickly but isn't sustainable if you want to keep quality and efficiency as you grow. There's always new research in AI that can make an existing service more accurate or power a new feature, and customers want to have Cognitive Services availability in more Azure regions, working with more languages and giving them more options to customize models.

To carry on scaling for more customers, with new services coming from research, as well as updates and operational maintenance to meet the Azure SLAs and deliver on certification, compliance, and data regulation obligations, the team created a single platform for Cognitive Services to run on, with the architecture you can see in Figure 9-1. There's also a single 24-7 support team with a rotating "Directly Responsible Individual" role;[1] someone who proactively looks at logs, responds to incidents, does root cause analysis, and assigns defects across all the services, so the demanding support role can be shared between more people. That level of

---

[1] Learn more about DRI (*https://go.microsoft.com/fwlink/?linkid=2190185*).

operational commitment is hard for even large enterprises to achieve when running their own AI systems.

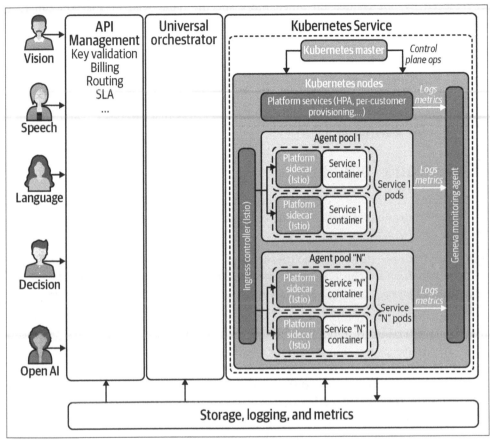

Figure 9-1. Running on a single platform makes Cognitive Services easier to update, operate, and scale; this is the architecture for Cognitive Services in a single Azure region

Building a more turnkey infrastructure makes Cognitive Services suitable for the "air-gapped" clouds required by some government contracts—where the operations team might not be experts in machine learning—but it also has other benefits. The completely automated deployment required for that means fewer errors in manual deployment anywhere the services are running, and faster disaster recovery. If an entire cluster needs to be rebuilt because something goes wrong, clicking a button runs the rebuild and sends traffic to the new cluster as soon as it's available.

Similarly, because those air-gapped deployments were on the same platform, features they required like private endpoints could be developed once and made available for the public cloud Cognitive Services too.

Using deep learning for all of the Cognitive Services models makes it straightforward to build custom models, where the final output layer of a trained deep neural network is replaced by one trained on much more specific data. That means you can take advantage of a model trained on a large dataset—which takes time—and quickly tweak it to handle your specific problem.

The Cognitive Services team also includes a group of researchers, known internally as Loonshots after the book about turning "crazy ideas" into successful projects, that shepherds new algorithms, models, and approaches from Microsoft Research—whose remit is to look two to three years ahead—into services that can be delivered within a year, all on the same platform.

Clusters and Containers

The architecture of the Cognitive Services platform uses containers running on Kubernetes (although it uses the same backend as the Azure Kubernetes Service, it's a separate deployment).

There are multiple clusters in each Azure region, each with its own VM agent pools; some services share clusters, while more demanding services like speech run on dedicated clusters.

The containers that run in Azure for Cognitive Services aren't the same containers that you can run at the edge to host specific Cognitive Services, because Microsoft takes advantage of the orchestrator it's built in the Cognitive Services platform to allocate different containers to different VM SKUs that might have GPUs and fast local storage or just CPUs. The different Cognitive Services are broken up into many microservices, and metadata defines what hardware and software requirements each of them needs, so the containers can be provisioned onto the appropriate infrastructure in the right agent pool. The container for one microservice might run on a low-power CPU, while another will be on a VM with a powerful GPU.

The orchestrator can send a request to one container to do, say, language detection as part of the text analytics service, and then forward that on to other containers for further processing. That fits with the way developers use multiple Cognitive Services together in scenarios like call center handling, where one cloud request can call multiple services, like speech, text analytics, language understanding, translation, and text-to-speech.

It's also how Applied AI Services like Forms Recognizer are composed: the orchestrator decomposes the customer request into multiple API calls to individual Cognitive Services behind the scenes and then merges them back together. That makes it easier to build and launch new Applied AI Services, because composing them is just metadata that the orchestrator can use.

The orchestrator also requires more standardization across the individual Cognitive Services APIs so the calls developers make to different APIs are more closely aligned. That means once you're familiar with one API, it's easier to understand the structure of new APIs as you start using them.

Using containers means fewer Linux VMs are needed to host Cognitive Services than if each service ran in its own VM. It's also faster and more efficient to scale.

Because of the time it takes to spin up an entire VM to handle increased traffic, a VM-based service will typically run with extra capacity as a buffer so customer requests are never dropped. Even running on Kubernetes, Cognitive Services still needs a certain amount of buffer capacity because, while it's fast to start up a new container, it still takes time to copy a large machine learning model into a new container. But that buffer can be even smaller because, rather than deploying the model into a new container, it can be kept outside and just attached once the container has scaled up.

Running Cognitive Services for so many customers means Microsoft gets a lot of telemetry that can be used to make running them more efficient. As different Azure VM SKUs become available or the prices of SKUs change, they can look at which VM to run a particular container on. Not all SKUs are available in all Azure regions; so while running on a VM with a GPU might give better performance for vision models, they also have to be able to run on CPU-only SKUs so they can be deployed in more regions.

That might mean going back not just to the developers who built that Cognitive Service but to the researchers and data scientists who created the model and to framework teams like ONNX to make sure the models and frameworks run on the variety of hardware in Azure. As new hardware becomes available, they can run performance and validation tests, spin up a new agent pool in the Kubernetes cluster, redeploy the service to that, and spin down the existing agent pool.

Making Cognitive Services not only scale but get cheaper and cheaper to run is key to making AI available to everyone. When the Edge browser added the ability to automatically translate web pages into a different language as they load, which you can see in action in Figure 9-2, it quickly became the biggest user of the Translator service—and the bill for running it went through the roof. Finding ways to bring the cost down by optimizing Translator to run on less powerful hardware in Azure meant the service could stay available in Edge and keep adding more languages.

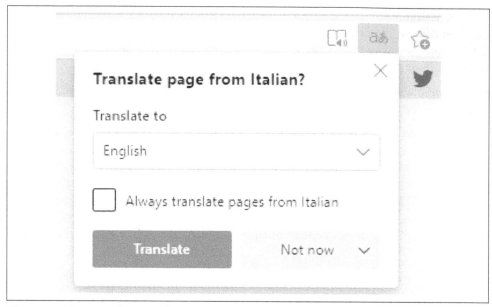

Figure 9-2. Putting the Translator service inside the Edge browser means Cognitive Services has to scale up to serve millions of users without breaking the bank

In this chapter we've looked at how cloud AI services are built, so you can be confident in relying on them for scale, as well as the trade-offs if you need to run any of the individual Cognitive Services in containers on your own infrastructure. But what does it look like to use Cognitive Services at scale in your own applications? In the next chapters we're going to look at some real-world examples of solving problems on mobile devices, at the edge, and in the cloud as examples of what you can build with the help of those AI services.

## CHAPTER 10

Seeing AI: Using Azure Machine Learning and Cognitive Services in a Mobile App at Scale

In previous chapters we've looked at how to use Azure Machine Learning and Cognitive Services. We've shown you how Microsoft runs Cognitive Services so it scales to massive numbers of users. But what does that look like inside a real-world application? What kind of architecture do you need to take advantage of Azure AI services? And how ambitious can you be when it comes to the kind of problems you can solve with AI services?

How about describing the world around them for millions of blind users, in real time?

In this chapter, we're going to look at how the Seeing AI app uses Azure Machine Learning and Cognitive Services to tell blind users what's in front of them, using a mix of prebuilt and custom models, running locally and in the cloud.

Think of the app as a talking camera: it can read out short sections of text like signs and labels, capture and recognize longer documents like forms and menus, and even read handwriting. It recognizes faces the user knows and describes the people around them; it can also describe what's in an image or narrate what's going on, like someone playing football in the park. It can describe a color, emit audio tones to describe how dark or bright it is, beep to help users scan a barcode to get information about the box or tin they're holding, and identify different bank notes when it's time to pay for something. Machine learning services on Azure provide the kind of descriptions shown in Figure 10-1, and the app delivers those in an interface designed specifically for its blind users.

Figure 10-1. Seeing AI uses Azure machine learning services to recognize objects and describe scenes

Custom and Cloud Models

That's a wide range of computer vision problems, so the app uses multiple machine learning models for the different scenarios and makes different trade-offs.

Running a machine learning model locally on the device gives you real-time results, ideally less than 100 milliseconds or at most under a quarter of a second, which means the user gets a responsive natural experience for having text read out to them.

But image description uses Custom Vision models in Cognitive Services that can't be compressed to run on the device, let alone the multigigabyte models trained in Azure Machine Learning to recognize many different types of objects. While the round trip to the cloud takes a little longer, it delivers higher quality.

If you want a sign or a label read out to you in real time, that's done with models running on the phone. But if you're taking a photo of a document rather than just holding up the phone, you're probably going to spend a few seconds getting a good picture, so it's worth taking the time to send that to Azure to take advantage of the very large models running in the cloud and get a more accurate result.

There are different ways to decide between running a model locally and in the cloud. Seeing AI does that by letting users choose different scenarios, but in your app you might decide based on factors like the speed of the internet connection or to take a hybrid approach. If someone has limited bandwidth, a slow connection, or is offline, you can use a local model—or even start giving them results using the small local model and then add more precise or accurate information as that comes back from the cloud. If you do that, make sure the user interface makes it clear why the quality or level of detail varies so the user isn't confused by seeing better results some of the time. You may also need to think about privacy; the images Seeing AI sends to Azure are stored securely and in a way that protects user privacy, but they do leave the device; if you're in a regulated industry where that's a problem, you may need to stick to local models—and if you are sending content to a cloud service, you may need to notify your users that's happening.

Image captioning in Seeing AI uses the Cognitive Services Vision API, and the Face API handles telling the user the age and gender of people. Object detection also uses Cognitive Services, with some models that need only fine-tuning trained using Custom Vision. For some scenarios, Seeing AI uses large models in the cloud that can recognize a lot of different objects, but as it introduces more augmented reality scenarios, that means running models that have been trained with Custom Vision and exported to run in CoreML for iOS and TensorFlow Lite on the device for the fastest response.

Other models that need full custom training, for scenarios like currency and barcodes, are built in Azure Machine Learning because these are so different from the everyday objects that prebuilt object detection models are trained on. The training images are uploaded to Azure Blob storage, the training scripts are run in Python using GPUs, and then a conversion script compresses the large model that's created into, again, CoreML or TensorFlow Lite. (If you need to target more platforms with your own applications, you can use ONNX, which we covered in Chapter 3.)

Choosing between Custom Vision and a custom object detection model built in Azure Machine Learning is about accuracy but also about model size.

Custom Vision is fast and convenient; it's much less work than building in Azure Machine Learning, and a general object decision model that recognizes people, animals, vehicles, and other everyday objects is accurate enough that it's not worth starting from scratch just to get slightly better results. The Seeing AI team trains the Custom Vision model using images of things their users need to have recognized that the standard object detection model might not be trained for, like stairs, elevators, building entrances, and doorways.

But the other factor is model size. The memory limitations on mobile devices limit how large a model can be, and a pretrained model like ImageNet is very generic and includes things that users aren't likely to come across frequently, like zebras and giraffes. Having those in the model doesn't make it less accurate at recognizing what Seeing AI users do care about, but it does mean the model is larger than it needs to be. The team is experimenting to see if it's worth training a model from scratch that covers the shorter list of objects they definitely need to recognize, like elements of the kind of buildings they want to navigate, because that creates a smaller model for a specific scenario.

Guided Tours

Using the LiDAR on recent iPhone models to build a 3D mesh of the world and combining that with object detection that uses the RGB camera to put bounding boxes around objects, Seeing AI can do audio augmented reality. The "world" feature is still in preview, but it can detect that there's a chair or a table, identify where in 3D space that furniture is, and then tell the user what it is using spatial audio to have that sound coming from the right location, to help them navigate around the table or sit down on the chair.

With custom models running locally on the device for real-time recognition, that can be even more powerful. With Azure Spatial Anchors, those virtual beacons can store more information: a light switch could say which lights in the room it controls. People could even attach information to help someone navigating through the office for the first time. A manager could record a route from reception to the kitchen to someone's desk, with audio breadcrumbs that will help a blind person move from waypoint to waypoint, something that could help get them back into the workplace without breaking social distancing guidelines.

The Seeing AI Backend

The infrastructure for the mobile Seeing AI app uses standard cloud design patterns for distributed applications. Whether it's Cognitive Services or any other cloud API, you don't want to put your API keys in your app; Seeing AI stores those secrets in Azure Key Vault and uses Azure AD to handle the connection to Key Vault. The easiest way to ensure a trusted connection between an app and the background service it connects to is to have to user log in; using Azure B2C lets you use the same architecture for handling users and managing secrets. That also simplifies using an Azure Web App or Azure Functions for telemetry and analytics, or if you want to cache results.

Images and other requests come in to the Seeing AI service from the app and fan out to the other services it uses. A backend service handles requests to multiple Cognitive

Services and combines the results from each service. That also allows Seeing AI to do load balancing and routing for Cognitive Services in different regions: you can do that with Azure Front Door for HTTP requests, which lets you do rate limiting and IP access control, or with Azure Traffic Manager if you need to route TCP or UDP traffic. Because the app is used in many countries and needs to talk to the closest Azure region to where the user is, the backend is configured to call the nearest instance of a Cognitive Service (and to fail over if that's not available). The backend also uses Azure Web Application Firewall to block malformed URIs that bad actors could use to attack the service.

Seeing AI doesn't need this, but if your backend is going to be used by different applications or if you want to offer different levels of service, you can use Azure API Management to rate limit different consumers.

Getting the Interface Right

The speed and accuracy of the Custom Vision and Azure Machine Learning models are what make Seeing AI useful, but they need to be wrapped in a good user experience to really be helpful. There's a key phrase in disability circles: "Nothing about us without us." Whoever your audience is, the results you get from Cognitive Services aren't useful unless the experience of the app is useful to them. Think about how users interact with the app and how you can give them the information they need to be productive.

If you're using Custom Vision or other options for customizing or personalizing the experience, make sure you allow users to give you feedback on how well that's working, so you can keep improving the results.

Remember that machine learning is inherently probabilistic rather than the usual binary "true or false" of coding. The results you get from machine learning models have confidence values to say how certain the model is they're correct. You have to think about error rates and be ready to handle confidence levels in your application without them being intrusive. Think about how you will handle the user experience if a result turns out to be wrong.

The descriptions of scenes in Seeing AI are phrased to make that clear, saying things like "it's probably a dog playing with a ball in the park."

For real-time scenarios, Seeing AI uses thresholds, and if the object detection service delivers a result that doesn't meet that threshold, it's not used. But because users are often moving around as they use the app, there might be multiple readings, so getting multiple observations may let you increase your confidence in other ways. You also need to handle those multiple results: it's important that Seeing AI doesn't say an object like a car has just appeared if it's actually the same car from a different angle.

Equally, you don't want to distract the user with notifications that aren't helpful or with descriptions that are too long to be useful. If further readings show an object is closer or farther away than it first seemed, Seeing AI will update the description but not interrupt the user to tell them that.

The key to getting the user experience right is understanding your users: what situation will they be in, what do they need from your application, and what will just get in their way? How will that look in the live experience, whether it's someone walking in the park or a camera monitoring a factory production line? Either will be quite different from wherever you do your coding, so as well as gathering a diverse set of training images, make sure to do plenty of testing with real users in their environment to have the best chance of making the results of your machine learning models really useful to them.

Whatever you're building your app to do, Seeing AI is a great example of how to use cloud AI services in a mobile app, including how to put together a cloud backend to orchestrate those services and when to use local models. As the name suggests, it concentrates on what can be seen in the world around you; in the next chapter, we'll look at working with speech. Suppose you need to not only transcribe but translate multiple languages while someone's talking: how close can you get to that science fiction classic—a real-time translation system?

## CHAPTER 11

Translating Multiple Languages at Scale for International Organizations

While many Azure Machine Learning and Cognitive Services applications are focused on business and consumer services, they're also important tools for governments and other public bodies. Machine learning–powered tools can help make organizations like these more efficient, removing bottlenecks and speeding up common processes. Microsoft has been championing these approaches, with initiatives like its AI for Good program.

One important role for Microsoft's AI tools is in breaking down barriers between different nationalities by providing tools for rapid, automatic translation. If you've used the captioning tools in PowerPoint or the Translator app on your smartphone, you're using tools built around Azure's speech recognition and translation services. We've looked at how to use them in your applications in Chapter 4, showing how speech recognition tools convert speech to text, how translation tools turn that text from one language to another, and how neural speech models deliver natural-sounding speech from translated text.

Delivering Translations for an International Parliament

Much of what we do with these tools is used to support individuals, translating menus or helping take a taxi across an unfamiliar city. But what if we need to provide near-real-time transcriptions of a large number of people, working in multiple languages, using a specialized vocabulary? That was the problem a team of Microsoft engineers had to solve in order to build a prototype translation service for the European Parliament, building on the same Cognitive Services APIs and tools we examined in Chapter 4.

Multinational bodies like the European Parliament work in many languages, with delegates from 27 countries speaking 24 different languages, and more than 4,000 interpreters. With no one official language, speeches needed both real-time transcriptions and translations, so that speakers could respond to speeches during debates while also creating an official record of proceedings. This means linking into the parliament sound and recording systems, automatically detecting languages and changing the transcription model on the fly as the language changes.

Connecting to Existing Audio-Visual (AV) Systems

A direct connection into the sound system wasn't possible due to the nature of the competitive tender, so systems had to work with a web API using MPEG-DASH. This added complexity, as MPEG-DASH delivers adaptive-rate audio data, while the Azure Cognitive Services inputs expect pulse-code modulation (PCM) audio streams encoded at 60K hertz. The audio system also delivered 25 different streams, one for each language and a main audio track from the parliament floor.

The Microsoft system had to first identify the live stream, then separate video and audio signals, before transcoding the audio track into PCM. Once separated, the two streams needed to be time coded, so the resulting transcriptions could be synchronized with the video stream before delivering it to end users. With a fixed requirement for less than seven seconds latency, there was limited time for the system to handle data conversions and deliver transcribed and translated captions.

Cloud native development techniques proved to be appropriate, using a microservice architecture to handle the initial signal processing using familiar open source tools like FFmpeg to manage transcoding before delivering the converted audio stream to the Cognitive Services translation tools. The real-time protocol SignalR was used to deliver the resulting captions back to the portal, along with time-coded offsets that were used to align the text with the original video streams. Latency remained low, the whole process taking less than two seconds.

Using Custom Speech Recognition for Specialized Vocabularies

As there was a significant amount of specialized vocabulary, Microsoft's Cognitive Services group worked to deliver a set of custom language models for the 24 required languages, using a dataset of speeches to train the models. Two teams worked on this aspect of the project, one handling transcription models and another on translations. The models were evaluated using their BLEU scores, which show how close to human translations their results were, as well as their word error rate. There was a minimum level for both scores that the models needed to beat.

Once trained, the custom models were made available through a private endpoint in Azure, with their own compute resources. This approach was no different from that available to anyone using Cognitive Services; the tools Microsoft used were the standard ones built into the platform.

The biggest issue facing the team building out the service was the quality of the incoming audio streams and the length of the overall audio pipeline. Each processing step adds latency, so you need to keep the number of steps to a minimum. There's also additional latency in the variable bit-rate web streams used as a source. A 32K stream could drop down to 5K and back up to 100K, before returning to its standard rate. While the prototype used software encoding to go from streams to an Azure-compatible format, in practice a hardware solution would have better performance and would keep latency to a minimum.

The software team also found that their initial container-based design was slower than using VMs to host their microservices. This was because the containers couldn't access GPU resources, while Azure provides GPU VMs. Switching from a serverless container host to infrastructure-as-a-service increases operating costs, but the gains in performance are significant. Like using hardware-based audio encoders, working with a limited latency budget means taking advantage of all the gains you can get from your hardware.

From Specialized Prototype to General Application

The same basic system has been white-labeled for use in different environments. One current proof of concept for another international body is being designed to work with in-meeting-room audio feeds using the popular Audinate Dante AV protocols. Here audio and video are delivered over Ethernet, using virtual sound cards to process the Dante audio stream. This meant rewriting the audio processor to handle alternate stream formats.

Here a .NET application running on a PC in the AV system takes the feed over Ethernet, using a virtual sound card from Audinate to get the audio channel. The app converts the sound data into a byte array that can then be delivered to Azure, either synchronously or using asynchronous processing techniques, depending on the requirements. Output data is delivered to a web portal, where it's presented as either a transcription or a real-time speech-to-speech translation. The real-time speech system is designed so that you can define a single output language, so that your stream is always in your chosen language. For example, a French speaker can choose their native language and have all translations delivered in French.

To translate a stream you first need to identify the language being spoken, then run the stream through the appropriate Cognitive Services APIs. With both parliamentary and committee meetings, there's an issue of rapid changes of speakers and languages. The system needed to be able to detect a change in language as soon as it happens, so that transcriptions are always in the right language. While the target is, again, the full 24 languages, initially it's starting with 10.

Working within Constraints

There's a lot to consider when going from a proof of concept like this service, which, while it could work at scale, wasn't fully tuned for full operations. A system like this needs to behave differently from a consumer service, as it needs to detect and remove vocal tics and pauses. It's also important to make sure you are accounting for regional variations in languages and understand the default settings in the underlying services.

For example, working in Europe you need to use PT-PT when translating Portuguese, not the default PT-BR, as Brazilian Portuguese has diverged from the original language. There's also a need for more targeted vocabularies, models that can be switched depending on context. A parliamentary session about economics will use a very different terminology from one about fishing policies or one about international aid.

There are also constraints that need to be considered: the requirement for GPU-enabled VMs will limit the Azure regions where a service like this can be run. Working outside a supported region may add additional latency that could vary unpredictably, even with a direct network connection into Azure. Similarly, it's important to stick to one hardware SKU for all your systems, as different processor generations handle machine learning data differently. For example, the high-efficiency BFLOAT instructions are only supported in recent server CPUs. Changing CPU to an older version will affect the accuracy of a model.

What's perhaps most interesting about Microsoft's work in delivering a set of tools that can handle multilanguage translation with minimal latency and high accuracy is that it uses off-the-shelf APIs and tools. There's no specialized research software running here; even where custom speech models are used, they're built and trained using the same APIs and portal that anyone can use. Even the underlying microservice model is a common cloud native design pattern, taking advantage of production Azure VM images and hardware.

Translation tools like this used to be science fiction but are now standard technologies available as APIs using common design patterns. These are tools anyone can use; the key to these projects was how Microsoft integrated them with existing AV systems. The same approach can be used in other environments.

## CHAPTER 12

Bringing Reinforcement Learning from the Lab to the Convenience Store

Nearly all the AI models and services we've covered so far have been based on supervised and semi-supervised machine learning, but a new technique called reinforcement learning has recently emerged from research labs to offer almost real-time learning.

Instead of looking for patterns in data, reinforcement learning systems learn by doing: training agents look at the context, make decisions, and get rewards as feedback. In the lab, reinforcement learning agents train inside games like Minecraft, where the context is the current state of the game, and there are a limited number of actions and clear rewards. In the real world, reinforcement learning can be useful for deciding what products to suggest to users,[1] what to have a bot say next, how to phrase an alert, which picture or video or ad to show—or any other optimization problem.

Azure uses reinforcement learning to decide the least disruptive time to reboot VMs that need to be reset or moved to a different physical server. Microsoft Teams uses it to determine what audio jitter buffer to use for every individual call. That buffer smooths out the way audio packets are handled to match any changes in the latency of the connection during the call, so the sound doesn't lag and you don't get dropouts when packets are delayed or choppy, mechanical-sounding speech as the system plays packets that arrive more quickly.

---

1 Find best practices for building recommendation systems with reinforcement learning in the Microsoft Recommenders GitHub repository (*https://go.microsoft.com/fwlink/?linkid=2190186*).

The Personalizer service (one of the Azure Cognitive Services we introduced in Chapter 4) is a single-step, single-decision optimization engine, and that single decision can be a lot of things.

The National Basketball Association is using Personalizer to make their app completely personalized to every user, showing them different articles and NBA highlight reels. You could use it to manage 5G configurations for phones connecting to a network, setting up the connection differently depending on whether it's likely to use more data or make more voice calls and based on the state of the 5G network at the time. Or you could manage loyalty programs, creating dynamic offers for how many repeat purchases customers have to make in what period of time to qualify for a reward, to get the right mix of benefits that keep customers happy but don't cost the store too much.

There's more and more personalization going on. When Microsoft first started using what became the Personalizer service internally, it solved a problem all machine learning models had failed on previously—placing news headlines on MSN—and improved click-through by 27%. The first year it was available, Personalizer handled 34 million transactions: the next year that was up to 11 billion, reaching 66 billion the year after. By the end of 2012, the service was handling over 9 billion personalization choices a month, inside Microsoft and for its customers.

The other advantage of reinforcement learning: because it's not based on historical patterns, it keeps working when habits change suddenly—the way they did at the start of the COVID-19 pandemic. Every machine learning model based on historical patterns stopped being relevant, but Personalizer was able to pick up on the changes, understanding user behavior in real time, training in real time, and updating the model in real time. It's also quick to build into your apps and workflows.

Two APIs, Eight Weeks, 100% Uplift

Anheuser-Busch InBev may be best known for Budweiser, but they have over 500 brands. To help bring those to smaller stores in Mexico, AB InBev set up an online marketplace called MiMercado. Initially, every store would see the same offers, but they might have very different customers and sales patterns. With a new business, there wasn't a lot of historical data to go on, and the development team wanted a plug-and-play system.

Even using Azure Machine Learning to run a simulation or manage the parallel learning that teaches reinforcement learning agents to make optimal decisions involves a certain level of complexity. Working with the Personalizer service means you only have two APIs to deal with, as shown in Figure 12-1.

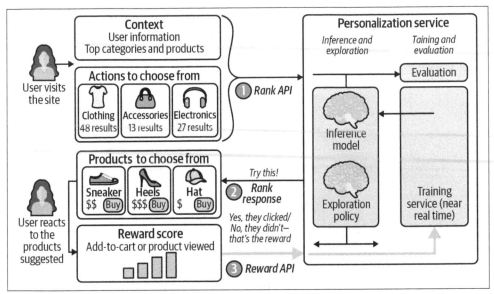

Figure 12-1. Working with the Decision service on a site like MiMercado is simple, and behind the scenes Cognitive Services ranks the choices, picks the best options, and handles the feedback loop to learn from that

Call the *Rank* API and pass in the context features—for MiMercado, that's everything AB InBev knows about the business and the user (a shopkeeper like the one in Figure 12-2)—along with the actions, which are all the product options and the context for those. The API returns which products to feature on the carousel, in which order. If the customer buys the product, the app calls the *Reward* API to send the reward, which updates the Personalizer model.

It was simple to build in to the online store app: it took just eight weeks from starting to having it in production. Using Personalizer doubled the number of times store owners clicked on recommendations and increased how often they actually ordered a featured product by two-thirds, adding up to 87% more orders per MiMercado user.

With supervised and semi-supervised learning, the more data you have, the better. Personalizer needs a certain amount of data and a reasonably fast turnaround on data points. If you have a remote industrial site where you can change a setting only once a month and you have to wait another month to see if the change made things better or worse, or if you're a very small online store, you're not going to get enough volume to be able to train even a reinforcement learning model. Ideally, you want things that happen at least 500 times a day. And if you have very high levels of traffic, Personalizer will be able to pick up on changes and trends more quickly because there will be enough signal in the volume of data to learn from in a matter of hours.

Figure 12-2. Using Personalizer to decide which products to show to small stores that use MiMercado led to a big jump in orders even as habits were changing

But you don't need to have a great many data points about users and situations, and you don't need any personal information. In fact, using too many features or data that's too precise just adds noise to the data, so Personalizer can help you adopt responsible AI approaches like using behavioral information rather than relying on PII or detailed user demographics like gender and age.

 Remember to make it clear to any users how personalization is being used—like a button titled *Why am I seeing these suggestions?* that shows the features and actions that influenced the results—and allow them to opt in or out of data collection.

It's more useful to know which group a user falls into—whether someone is using a Mac, a Windows PC, or a phone, and how much battery their device has left—than to know who they are. If it's a shopping site, knowing what categories they've purchased recently and their average spend is better than their entire shopping history. Knowing what region they're in is more useful than knowing their address, and it's better to record if it's a workday or the weekend and morning, afternoon, evening, or night than to send the time down to the second.

The more precise the data, the sparser and more unique it is, making it harder to learn from; avoiding personal information makes it denser and more useful. The same is true for the context you send. Giving the color and price band for pairs of shoes and saying what they're made of is more useful than the exact price and the model number. You might want to include metadata like how old a video or news story is, or process it through other Cognitive Services, like using Computer Vision or Text Analytics to extract who is featured.

Personalizer is adding the option to look at historical data to help you choose how to bucket data into features, as well as telling you which features in your data are most useful, slightly useful, or completely irrelevant. (That's handy if you think something should make a difference but doesn't, because it might mean you're not telling people about it well enough.)

But if you only have two or three pieces of data for each context and action and a handful of data points about your users, Personalizer can still give you excellent results.

 You might need to do more work if you have large numbers of actions or products to choose from. At the time of writing, Personalizer can handle only 50 choices; in the future it may be able to help you with filtering or classifying more options down to those choices.

The improvement you'll see is usually significant, with typical results ranging from doubling usage or sales up to four-digit improvements.

In many ways, Personalizer is the perfect example of Azure AI services. It's based on decades of research into techniques that have only recently become robust enough to be used in production, are still complex to set up, require strong data science skills, and are evolving rapidly as research continues. But what you get is a robust system that's proven in production and can handle enormous scale, with minimal development effort, even if you have little data science expertise. That's cloud AI in action.

If what you've learned so far has whetted your appetite and you're ready to apply Azure AI services to your own business problems, read on for a little help getting started.

Afterword

By now, you should have a good understanding of what you can do with cloud AI, but there are plenty of resources to help you as you work with Azure AI services.

The best way to get started (if you haven't already) is to sign up for an Azure account (turn back to Chapter 2 for a reminder of how to do that) and start trying out some of the steps in previous chapters. If you don't want to type in the code samples, remember that you can find the full code we've excerpted them from in our GitHub repository (*https://oreil.ly/tCRAU*).

Microsoft has comprehensive documentation, including tutorials, quickstarts, links to GitHub repositories with templates, sample code and projects, and even sandboxes where you can try out code for some services. Try the interactive AI demos (*https://aidemos.microsoft.com*), or learn more about specific services:

- Azure Machine Learning (*https://go.microsoft.com/fwlink/?linkid=2190248*)
- Cognitive Services (*https://go.microsoft.com/fwlink/?linkid=2190251*)
- Applied AI Services (*https://go.microsoft.com/fwlink/?linkid=2190264*)
- All the Azure AI and machine learning services (*https://go.microsoft.com/fwlink/?linkid=2190131*)
- Power Platform (*https://go.microsoft.com/fwlink/?linkid=2190138*)
- Logic Apps (*https://go.microsoft.com/fwlink/?linkid=2190133*)

There are also courses on Microsoft Learn with tutorials, videos, code samples, and sandboxes where you can try out key techniques (and gain credits toward certifications like Azure AI Fundamentals (*https://go.microsoft.com/fwlink/?linkid=2190255*)). Start with the AI School (*https://www.microsoft.com/en-us/ai/ai-school*) or explore specific learning paths for AI (*https://go.microsoft.com/fwlink/?linkid=2190245*).

If you're looking for datasets to try the various Azure AI services out on, Azure Open Datasets include public domain data for weather, census, holidays, public safety, and location that are hosted on Azure, integrated in Azure Machine Learning, and accessible through APIs so you can use them with Cognitive Services or in the Power Platform. View the catalog (*https://go.microsoft.com/fwlink/?linkid=2190262*). You may also want to look at the Microsoft Research Open Data (*https://msropen data.com/datasets*) repository of more specialized research datasets Microsoft has created in various areas of science, including healthcare and education.

If you need help with using Azure AI services or you want to chat with fellow developers, there are communities on Stack Overflow for many of the services:

- Azure Machine Learning Service (*https://oreil.ly/9jbYq*)
- Power BI (*https://go.microsoft.com/fwlink/?linkid=2190130*)
- Power Automate (*https://go.microsoft.com/fwlink/?linkid=2190137*)
- Power Apps (*https://go.microsoft.com/fwlink/?linkid=2190134*)
- Azure Logic Apps (*https://go.microsoft.com/fwlink/?linkid=2190142*)
- Microsoft Cognitive Services (*https://go.microsoft.com/fwlink/?linkid=2190132*)
- Microsoft Translator (*https://go.microsoft.com/fwlink/?linkid=2190136*)
- Microsoft Custom Vision (*https://go.microsoft.com/fwlink/?linkid=2190135*)
- Microsoft Speech API (*https://go.microsoft.com/fwlink/?linkid=2190140*)
- Microsoft Speech Platform (*https://go.microsoft.com/fwlink/?linkid=2190141*)
- Bot Framework (*https://go.microsoft.com/fwlink/?linkid=2190252*)
- Azure Language Understanding (*https://oreil.ly/bD3eZ*)
- Azure Cognitive Search (*https://go.microsoft.com/fwlink/?linkid=2190146*)

You can also connect with almost 150 Microsoft MVPs (*https://oreil.ly/BnxCB*) around the world who specialize in AI and blog, present, run workshops, build tools and sample apps showing off the various Azure AI services—and can help you out if you get stuck.

If this book has piqued your interest in some of the underlying AI techniques, there's a wealth of information on the Microsoft Research site (*https://go.microsoft.com/fwlink/?linkid=2190147*), including research papers, webinars, and events like the Microsoft Research Summit. For a higher-level view, check out the AI topics on the Microsoft Research Blog (*https://go.microsoft.com/fwlink/?linkid=2190242*). Or if you need some inspiration for what can be achieved with AI, check out the Microsoft AI site (*https://www.microsoft.com/en-us/ai*).

Whatever you want to build, remember that AI is a tool—to apply it well, you need to really understand the problem that you're solving. Whatever service you use, whatever models you train, start by thinking about what you or your users need to be successful, measure what AI can deliver against that, and you'll be able to use the Azure AI services to make your apps smarter, more useful, easier to use, or just more fun to use.

Index

ONNX Runtime, 18
OpenAI, 5, 86
  (see also Azure OpenAI Service)
  Azure OpenAI Service, 61-64
  GPT-3 large language models, 5
  measuring accuracy of results for, 168
OpenVINO, 28
optical character recognition (see OCR)
optimization techniques, 5
orchestrator (containers), 176
overfitting of data models, 167

P
Pandas data analysis library, 48, 74
parallelism technologies, 5
performance metrics, establishing, 167-168
personal or sensitive information, data containing, 162
personalization, 190
  clear reasons for use of, 192
Personalizer service, 75, 189-193
personally identifiable information (PII), 76
planning processes for AI projects, 147
Power AI
Power Apps, 17, 86, 103
  AI Builder feature, 17, 104
  combining with Power Automate, 134
  using AI Builder models in, 123
Power Apps Studio, 113
  integrating AI Builder models in, 125
Power Automate, 17, 86, 103
  AI Builder feature, 104
  Cognitive Services integration, 105
  using AI Builder models in, 119
    Document Automation starter kit, 123
  using Cognitive Services and other AI models in, 126-134
    combining Power Apps and Power Automate, 134
    custom connectors, 131
Power BI, 16, 17, 22, 103
  AI features used in, 104, 105-113
    AI visualizations, 107-109
    building your own custom models for, 111-113
    offering appropriate tools to different levels of users, 106
    using AI for data preparation, 109

    working with custom Machine Learning models, 110
    running Python and R scripts and importing datasets from, 111
    shared data from, 160
    Video Analyzer player widget, 82
Power Platform, 13, 104-105
  AI Builder, 113, 119
  custom connectors in, 131
  dependence on and integration with other services, 104
  details on AI capabilities in services, 17
  no, low, and pro code, 105
  support for Cognitive Services APIs in, 22
Power Query, 109, 110
Power Query Editor, 109, 110, 112
Power Virtual Agents, 104
precision and recall, 168
prediction models in AI Builder, 113, 115
predictions
  exploring with use of counterfactuals, 149
  human oversight and, 153
principles of least privilege, 163
privacy concerns in AI, 143
professional developers, relevance of Power Platform, 105
programming languages
  support by Visual Studio Code editor, 14
  supported by Cognitive Services, 51, 52
prompts (for GPT-3 models), 62
prosody, 50
provenance of data, 160
Python
  Azure Machine Learning Python SDK, 31
  Azure Machine Learning SDK for local development, 33-35
  Cognitive Services support for, 51
  logging tools in Azure Machine Learning, 45
  support by Visual Studio Code editor, 33
  using Azure Machine Learning studio with Notebooks and, 39-41
  using with anomaly detector, 74
  using with Azure Machine Learning studio, 31
Python SDK, 22
PyTorch, 28, 32
  using with Azure Machine Learning and TensorFlow, 41-43

About the Authors

Simon Bisson has been a freelance technology writer since the '90s, covering everything from start-ups and consumer gadgets to small business technology to enterprise architectures to developer tools and application development. In what he sometimes describes as "career as verb rather than noun," he moved into IT from academic, military, and telecom research (sometimes all three at once), running the technology side of one of the UK's first national ISPs and working as a consultant on many early ecommerce sites, with a natural progression into journalism to explain to other people how to do similar things. He still writes code (currently building aircraft tracking tools for Raspberry Pi), though he's just as likely to be taking photographs and maybe, just maybe, finishing a science fiction short story.... Find him on Twitter as @sbisson.

Mary Branscombe completed an MSc in intelligent knowledge-based systems in 1990. She was then convinced that, as promising as the AI techniques she'd been studying were, they weren't even close to being ready. Since then, she's been a technology journalist covering the rise of Windows, the birth of the web and smartphones, and, most recently, the arrival of AI as techniques mainstream developers can take advantage of. When not working, she can be found absorbed in a book, traveling (in more normal times), making a fuss of her cats, cooking something with a lot of garlic, thinking about taking up pottery again, or finishing the knitting, embroidery, and patchwork quilts she's been working on for the last umpteen years. She also dabbles in mystery fiction about the world of technology and start-ups, she really does have a USB earring, and you can find her almost any time on Twitter: @marypcbuk.

Chris Hoder works on the Cognitive Services team at Microsoft and is a lead product manager for the Azure OpenAI Service, which provides API-based access to OpenAI's large language models. He is responsible for the overall developer experience, from UI design to API and SDK experiences. Previously, he drove the end-to-end developer experience across the entire suite of Cognitive Services focused on API design, engagement, and retention. Before joining the Cognitive Services team, Chris worked directly with customers to envision, design, build, and deploy AI-focused applications using Microsoft's AI stack.

Anand Raman leads program management for the AI Services Platform at Microsoft. Previously, he was the chief of staff for the Microsoft Azure AI and Data Group, covering data platforms and machine learning, and ran the company's product management and the development teams for Azure Data Services and the Visual Studio and Windows Server user experience teams; he also worked several years as a researcher before joining Microsoft. Anand holds a PhD in computational fluid mechanics.

Colophon

The animal on the cover of *Azure AI Services at Scale for Cloud, Mobile, and Edge* is a tokay gecko (*Gekko gecko*). This arboreal gecko is native to Asia and some Pacific islands like the Philippines and throughout the Indo-Australian archipelago.

At 10–12 inches long, the tokay gecko is thought to be the third largest of the true geckos. There are two variants: red-spotted and black-spotted. Both have blue-gray skin but they can change their skin color to better blend in with their environment.

Tokay geckos eat insects, vegetation, and small vertebrates. When young geckos hatch, they feed on the outer covering of their own skin. Juveniles will sometimes prey upon geckos of the same species.

When threatened, the tokay gecko can detach its tail in defense. The tail will regenrate in about three weeks but the regenerated tail is usually shorter than the original.

These lizards are known for their sticky grip, which allows them to hang onto a vertical surface with only one toe. Fine filaments on the pads of their feet, known as setae, form molecular bonds with walls and ceilings.

A unique feature of this gecko is its rudimentary third eye, which is also found in the diurnal species of two reptile orders. Although they cannot see from this eye, it is highly sensitive to light and may help regulate activity in certain light conditions.

Tokay geckos are aggressive and have a strong bite. They are common in the illegal pet trade, but their bite makes them difficult to handle when caught as adults. They can live about 15–20 years.

According to folklore in some East Asian countries, these geckos have descended from dragons. They are a symbol of good luck and fertility. However, in some parts of Asia, the geckos are poached for medicinal uses.

The tokay gecko's conservational status is Least Concern. Many of the animals on O'Reilly covers are endangered; all of them are important to the world.

The cover illustration is by Karen Montgomery, based on an antique line engraving from Adobe Stock. The cover fonts are Gilroy Semibold and Guardian Sans. The text font is Adobe Minion Pro; the heading font is Adobe Myriad Condensed; and the code font is Dalton Maag's Ubuntu Mono.